WEST

MEETS

EAST

ASCD MEMBER BOOK

Many ASCD members received this book as a
member benefit upon its initial release.

Learn more at: **www.ascd.org/memberbooks**

WEST MEETS EAST

Best Practices from Expert
Teachers in the U.S. and China

Alexandria, Virginia, USA

Leslie **Grant** \ James **Stronge** \ Xianxuan **Xu** \ Patricia **Popp** \ Yaling **Sun** \ Catherine **Little**

1703 N. Beauregard St. • Alexandria, VA 22311-1714 USA
Phone: 800-933-2723 or 703-578-9600 • Fax: 703-575-5400
Website: www.ascd.org • E-mail: member@ascd.org
Author guidelines: www.ascd.org/write

Gene R. Carter, *Executive Director;* Richard Papale, *Acting Chief Program Development Officer;* Stefani Roth, *Interim Publisher;* Genny Ostertag, *Acquisitions Editor;* Julie Houtz, *Director, Book Editing & Production;* Jamie Greene, *Editor;* Dayna Elefant, *Senior Graphic Designer;* Mike Kalyan, *Manager, Production Services;* Circle Graphics, Inc., *Typesetter*

PAPERBACK ISBN: 978-1-4166-1820-1   ASCD product #111012

ASCD Member Book No. FY14-6B (Apr. 2014, PS). ASCD Member Books mail to Premium (P), Select (S), and Institutional Plus (I+) members on this schedule: Jan, PSI+; Feb, P; Apr, PSI+; May P; Jul, PSI+; Aug, P; Sep, PSI+; Nov, PSI+; Dec, P. For up-to-date details on membership, see www.ascd.org/membership.

Also available as an e-book (see Books in Print for the ISBNs).

Quantity discounts: 10–49 copies, 10%; 50+ copies, 15%; 1,000+, special discounts (e-mail program team@ascd.org or call 800-933-2723, ext. 5773, or 703-575-5773). Also available in e-book formats. For desk copies, go to www.ascd.org/deskcopy.

Library of Congress Cataloging-in-Publication Data

Grant, Leslie.
  West meets East : best practices from expert teachers in the U.S. and China / Leslie Grant, James Stronge, Xianxuan Xu, Patricia Popp, Yaling Sun, Catherine Little.
    pages cm.
  Includes bibliographical references and index.
    ISBN 978-1-4166-1820-1 (pbk. : alk. paper) 1. Effective teaching—United States. 2. Effective teaching—China. 3. Comparative education. I. Stronge, James. II. Xu, Xianxuan. III. Popp, Patricia A. IV. Sun, Yaling. V. Little, Catherine. VI. Title.
    LB1025.3.G724 2014
    371.102—dc23
                         2013049284

23 22 21 20 19 18 17 16 15 14   1 2 3 4 5 6 7 8 9 10 11 12

WEST MEETS EAST

Best Practices from Expert Teachers in the U.S. and China

Acknowledgments
致谢

Work on this book has been a highly collaborative and international endeavor. We wish to thank the many schools and their administrators for opening their doors and welcoming us, despite the extra time and paperwork such visits entailed. Furthermore, we would like to thank our universities, The College of William and Mary School of Education, Yunnan Normal University, and the University of Connecticut, for their support of this project, which allowed us to travel to each other's country and experience each other's culture. The desire to understand each other more fully was very mutual, and the relationships that have been established continue to grow. In addition, we have the great fortune of working with many graduate students who have made significant contributions to the book. Specifically, we thank Jessica Straessle for her research review on instructional planning, which was woven into Chapter 3. In addition, we thank Genny Ostertag and Jamie Greene from ASCD for their unwavering support and keen suggestions that contributed substantially to the quality of the book.

Most important, we wish to express our most sincere appreciation to the inspirational teachers who graciously opened their classrooms and thought processes to us for this study.

A middle school math teacher in China had prepared a work-sheet for her students with a sketch of a flower in the top corner. We were told that it was a flower endemic to China called Wintersweet. "This flower blooms in winter. In Chinese culture, it is a symbol of bravery, integrity, and perseverance. This communicates the teachers' expectations for their students to be brave to face the challenges that life holds or the challenges they will encounter in learning. It is a strategy for motivation."

The teachers represented in this book were wonderful models for their students. They demonstrated the willingness to continually grow and change practices to meet the needs of ever-changing students. Wintersweet may well be used as a symbol for these teachers!

1

Introduction and Overview
第一章 : 引论和纵览

The impact of globalization is rapidly posing new and demanding challenges to individuals and societies. In this globalized world, people compete for jobs—not just locally but also internationally. At the Microsoft Partners in Learning Global Forum on November 8, 2011, U.S. Secretary of Education Arne Duncan acknowledged that "education and global job markets are much more competitive today than even a generation ago," but he also noted that educators and nations need to work together to advance "achievement and attainment everywhere" (U.S. Department of Education, 2012, p. 1). Inherent in this statement is the notion that schools and students in the United States must remain competitive in order to support tomorrow's economy and American prosperity. Developing new cohorts of highly qualified and competitive workers requires a high-quality education system in every local community.

The United States must remain competitive globally, but it also needs to ensure that graduates have the skills necessary to enter a workforce that didn't even exist when they started school. Employment in the professional, scientific, technical, and computer systems fields—all fields that rely heavily on logic, reasoning, and critical thinking—is expected to increase by 45 percent by 2018 (U.S. Department of Labor, 2010).

Education expert Tony Wagner has conducted scores of interviews with business leaders and observed hundreds of classes in some of the nation's most highly regarded public schools (Wagner, 2008). As a result, he discovered a profound disconnect between what employers look for in potential employees (critical thinking skills, problem-solving skills, collaboration, creativity, and effective communication) and what our schools provide (passive learning environments and uninspired lesson plans that focus on test preparation and reward memorization). He notes that this problem exists not only in low-performing schools but also in top schools where skills that matter most in the global knowledge economy are not being taught or tested. (By *global knowledge economy,* we refer to the keen and growing competition across the world for high-end jobs—especially in the service sector—that are dependent on highly educated, creative individuals who can fulfill the requirements of the work and, more important, create new job opportunities.) Young people in the United States are effectively being equipped to work in job fields that are quickly disappearing from the economy, whereas young adults in countries such as India and China are competing for the world's most sought-after careers. We simply cannot afford this disconnect between what is taught in U.S. schools and what is required in the globally connected workplace.

Over the last two to three decades, while other countries have made significant improvements to their education systems, the United States has made only incremental changes. As a consequence, students in the United States lag in academic performance when compared with their peers in other industrialized nations, particularly in science and mathematics. The United States ranks well below places such as South Korea, Finland, Singapore, Hong Kong (a special administrative region of China), Shanghai (a province-level city under direct control of the Chinese central government), Japan, New Zealand, Australia, and Canada. The 2012 Organisation for Economic Co-operation and Development Programme for International Student Assessment indicated that, of the 34 countries evaluated, the United States ranked 17th in reading, 21st in science, and 26th in mathematics (OECD, 2013). Twenty-sixth in math!

In this the-world-is-flat era, the United States and China demand more competitive human capital and, therefore, sustained investment in and development of human capacity. For the last few decades, such investment has been emphasized as an important factor contributing to economic growth. Continuous improvement of educational opportunities for young people is one of the best means of human capital investment, and it carries an enormous potential for payback. This is seen in improved student development and performance in order to master the skills that are necessary to compete globally (Baker, Goesling, & LeTendre, 2002; Chudgar & Luschei, 2009). For many years, researchers, policymakers, and educational practitioners in both the United States and China have explored the variables that impact student achievement. The issue of teacher quality has been the focus of discussion and debate time after time, since the classroom teacher is widely regarded as the most influential school-related factor that affects student achievement (Mendro, Jordan, Gomez, Anderson, & Bembry, 1998; Muijs & Reynolds, 2003; Stronge, Ward, & Grant, 2011). Teacher effectiveness is the pillar of educational policy agendas, and it mediates the impact that any instruction-related reform or intervention has on student learning (Stronge, 2010).

What is important for U.S. educators (indeed, for educators in any nation) to understand is that, even though we may be making incremental reforms and improvements, we aren't competing against a stationary goal. Rather, as educators in one country seek to improve, so do educators around the world. Thus, we're always aiming at a moving target. We must get better—substantially better—if we want to remain competitive and successful moving forward. Make no mistake—this is a highly competitive world in which we live and work.

Educational Reform

China

On the other side of the globe, China has undertaken a nationwide program of curriculum reform since 2001. This reform is considered to be one of the most ambitious and far-reaching changes to schooling in recent Chinese history (Sargent, 2006). In addition to an overhaul of the objectives and content of curriculum materials, it calls for a paradigm shift in educational philosophy and a corresponding transformation in teaching practices at the classroom level. This represents a significant shift away from the traditional

Chinese model—which focused primarily upon memorization, drilling, and prescribed textbooks—to practices that foster individuality, self-expression, inquiry, and creative thinking skills. The traditional education system in China is often criticized for encouraging conformity, being highly examination-oriented, discouraging the development of students' creativity, and bolstering authoritarian teachers for whom the rigid and centralized curriculum is a more important agenda than catering to individual differences among students (Cheng, 2004).

Preus (2007) observed that the national education reform movement in China has moved its educational system toward a decentralization of elementary and secondary education. The central government has taken steps toward loosening its control over curriculum and assessment. For instance, the government used to have complete control over the development and selection of textbooks. Under new guidelines intended to stimulate innovation and creativity, teachers at the provincial, local, and school levels are beginning to enjoy the autonomy to develop and select textbooks. Overall, China is striving to establish a "quality-oriented" rather than a "test-oriented" system. Guidelines for this nationwide reform (drafted by the Ministry of Education) call for changes that are represented in Figure 1.1.

Already, these reforms are paying off. Shanghai is new to international assessment, but the city significantly outperformed even top-performing nations in all three subjects (OECD, 2010). As one of the most internationalized cities in China, Shanghai has been at the forefront of the country's educational reform. Although Shanghai cannot represent the whole country, its success indicates that China's move away from its traditional examination-driven system and to a system that aims to equip students with 21st-century skills is on track.

The educational system in Shanghai—and in China at large—has undergone several stages of development: the rigid Russian model during the 1950s, a period of "renaissance" in the early 1960s, disastrous damage during the Cultural Revolution (1966–1976), rapid expansion of basic education during the 1980s and 1990s, and in the 21st century a move toward higher education that is widely accessible to students across the entire country (OECD, 2010).

For readers who are not familiar with traditional Chinese culture or its customs, we would like to digress here to describe briefly what conventional

| FIGURE 1.1 | Nationwide Reform Changes in China |

Moving Away From . . .	Moving Toward . . .
Transmitting pure knowledge	Fostering learning attitudes and values
Discipline-based knowledge	More comprehensive and balanced learning experiences
"Bookish" knowledge	Relevance and interest of the content in the curriculum
Repetitive and mechanistic rote learning	Increased student participation, real-life experience, capacity in communications and teamwork, and an ability to acquire new knowledge and analyze and solve problems
Deemphasizing the screening and selective functions of assessments	Emphasizing the formative and constructive functions of assessments
Centralization of curriculum and learning experiences	Adaptation of curriculum and learning experiences to local relevance and needs

Chinese classroom teaching looks like. Observers of Chinese classrooms share a common impression—namely, large class sizes with students sitting in rows of desks facing the teacher and the teacher leading nearly all of the classroom activities and doing most of the talking to reticent students (Fang & Gopinathan, 2009; Huang & Leung, 2004; Paine, 1990). It has been well documented that teaching in Chinese culture is defined by demonstration, modeling, repeated drilling, and memorization (Jin & Cortazzi, 2008).

Western observers of classroom instruction in China are also usually impressed by the discipline and concentrated attention of Chinese students, along with the rapid pace and intensity of teacher-centered interaction (Jin & Cortazzi, 2008; Marton, Dall'Alba, & Kun, 1996). Typically, classes in China are large—in excess of 50 students—and classroom interaction is teacher-centered and text-based. Instructional methods are largely expository, and they are overtly driven by external high-stakes examinations (Biggs, 1996; Cortazzi & Jin, 1996). The teacher is often deemed to be an authoritative model—someone who has expert knowledge and skills, upstanding moral behavior, and an answer for every question. With respect to students, they are quiet and careful listeners (Jin & Cortazzi, 2008). Paine (1990) described Chinese lessons as dominated by teacher talk. Teachers act as artistic performers, and students are the audience.

Such a learning environment is opposite to the ideal learning environment defined in Western literature. Western intuitive thinking would perceive that Confucian-heritage culture results in rote learning and low student achievement (Biggs, 1996). However, students of Asian origin have been able to excel on international examinations. This phenomenon has attracted much attention since the 1980s (e.g., Stevenson, Lee, & Stigler, 1986; Stevenson & Stigler, 1992; Stigler, Lee, Lucker, & Stevenson, 1982; Sue & Okazaki, 1990). It seems that the strategy of memorization used by Chinese students is not simply for rote learning but an important method to achieve a deep understanding in which subject content is internalized and actively reflected upon (Watkins & Biggs, 1996, 2001).

Teacher authority and suppression of individual expression are deeply rooted in Confucian and collectivistic cultures (Ho, 2001). In Chinese classrooms, there is a high expectation for members to conform to a uniform standard of behavior. Unlike Western cultures, where harmonious social relations rest upon the satisfaction of individual needs or rights and fairness to all, "proper behavior in the Confucian collectivistic culture is defined by social roles, with mutual obligation among members of society and the fulfillment of their duties for each other being emphasized" (Ho, 2001, p. 100). Another characteristic of Chinese education is its emphasis on basic knowledge and skills. Chinese teachers and learners tend to believe that basic skills are fundamental and must precede any effort to encourage higher-level learning (Cheng, 2004; Soh, 1999).

In Chinese culture, learning is believed to occur through continual, careful shaping and modeling, and higher-order learning—such as analysis, evaluation, and creativity—is demonstrated only after the child has perfected prescribed and approved performances (Cheng, 2004). Whole-class instruction is the prevailing strategy, and the teacher is perceived to be the "purveyor of authoritarian information" (Stevenson & Stigler, 1992, p. 18), transmitting knowledge through repetition and rote memorization to students who act as passive recipients. These characteristics of Chinese classrooms are in sharp contrast to what is found to be conducive to student learning in Western academics.

In U.S. classrooms, learning activities are much more student-centered, with teachers acting as facilitators and students actively participating in individual or group work. The focus on individualism found in Western culture suggests that learning is optimal when student self-expression is exploited and when students are engaged in exploration. In the West, educators believe that students learn best when they begin by exploring and then move to an understanding of concepts and development of skills. However, educators in China believe that understanding content must occur before creative exploration of the learned concepts (Biggs, 1996).

It is also worth mentioning that Western and Chinese theories about the dichotomy of nature versus nurture are also different. Generally, Chinese culture credits nurture over nature in human learning and achievement. The Confucian philosophy of learning and achievement places primary emphasis on nonintelligence factors—such as personality traits (e.g., motivation, perseverance, effort) and environmental factors (e.g., parental and familial support, teacher and school instruction)—rather than natural ability as the most important prerequisites for desired performance (Chen & Stevenson, 1995; Rosenthal & Feldman, 1991; Shi & Zha, 2000).

Confucius's lasting influence in history resides in his concept of *ren* (仁), which is "a lifelong striving for any human being to become the most genuine, sincere, and humane person he or she can become" (Li, 2003, p. 146). According to Confucius, the process of actualizing ren is a process of self-cultivation and self-perfection. He taught that the goal for an individual is the development of personality until the ideal of a perfect man, a true gentleman or sage, has been reached. Confucius believed that, within this developmental process, one's single-minded effort and consistent practice are more important than one's innate ability to achieve success (Tweed & Lehman, 2002). Ultimately, ideal status of ren is achievable by anyone striving for it.

Chinese teachers influenced by Confucian thinking tend to regard the possibility of overachieving or underachieving as under one's individual control rather than being predestined by natural ability. Research also reveals that Chinese and Western cultures have different attribution patterns and loci of control (Hau & Salili, 1991; Salili & Hau, 1994; Walberg, 1992). People from Chinese cultures tend to attribute success to effort and failure to lack of effort, whereas people from Western cultures tend to attribute success *and* failure to ability (or lack thereof). Gardner (1995) made the following comment regarding the phenomenon that East Asian students outscored their U.S. counterparts on IQ tests:

> Genetics, heredity, and measured intelligence play no role here. East Asian students learn more and score better on just about every kind of measure because they attend school for more days, work harder in school and at home after school, and have better-prepared teachers and more deeply engaged parents who encourage and coach them each day and night. Put succinctly, Americans believe (like Herrnstein and Murray) that if you do not do well, it is because they lack talent or ability; Asians believe it is because they do not work hard enough. (p. 31)

United States

With the passing and implementation of No Child Left Behind (NCLB) in 2001, the U.S. federal government emphasized the need for states and school districts to ensure that *all* students—particularly at-risk students, students who are ethnically and linguistically marginalized, or students who are otherwise disadvantaged—have access to "highly qualified teachers." The NCLB law used three key guidelines to determine whether a teacher is highly qualified: (1) at least a bachelor's degree in the subject taught, (2) full state teacher certification, and (3) demonstrated knowledge in the subject taught (U.S. Department of Education, 2001).

The notion of effective teachers, as reflected in U.S. educational policies, has evolved considerably. For most of the 20th century, when candidates completed a state-approved teacher preparation program, they were eligible for teacher certification. In the 1980s, several states implemented performance assessments to ensure that teachers were equipped with a uniform set of competencies regardless of the content areas or grade levels they taught. Those competencies were largely drawn from process-product research on teaching and were perceived to be evidence-based. During the past 10 years, the standards used to assess teacher effectiveness have increasingly reflected the real complexities of classroom teaching. In particular, they emphasize the context-specific nature of teaching and the need for teachers to integrate knowledge of subject matter, students, and contextual conditions as they make instructional decisions, engage students in learning, and reflect on practice (Wayne & Youngs, 2003).

In order to improve the quality of schools and positively affect students' lives, teaching quality must be addressed. This is our best hope to improve education as a whole both systematically and dramatically. Curriculum can be reformed, but, ultimately, teachers must implement it. Professional development on new instructional strategies can be provided, but, ultimately, teachers must incorporate them into their instruction. There can be an increased focus on data analysis of student performance, but, ultimately, teachers must produce the results (Stronge, 2011). The highest-achieving countries around the world have committed significant resources to teacher training and support over the last decade. They raised standards and created stronger pathways for teacher education, providing teachers with more content and pedagogical knowledge. They paid their teachers well in relation to competing occupations, and they provided teachers with meaningful time for professional learning (Darling-Hammond, 2010).

In the early 1970s, less than half of all students in Singapore reached 4th grade. In the 1960s, only 1 in 10 adults completed more than nine years of basic education in Finland. What made a difference in the powerful turnaround in these educational systems? The answer is largely found in government policies, which identified and nurtured high-quality teachers. One of the lessons learned is that the quality of an education system cannot exceed the quality of its teachers (Barber & Mourshed, 2007). The educational reform initiatives in the so-called Asian tiger countries—Singapore, Shanghai, and South Korea—have become more "American" and have become increasingly learner-centered and focused on higher-order thinking. (As previously indicated, Shanghai is not a separate nation but rather a province-level city under the direct control of the central government in China. It also is the most populous metropolitan area in the country, with a population of approximately 23 million people. For international educational comparative purposes of this review, Shanghai was treated as a separate entity in the latest PISA data.) Although it has a long way to go, the Chinese Ministry of Education in now attempting to follow a path for learner innovation and creativity in the nationwide curriculum.

The educational system in the United States needs to stay innovative in order to rediscover its competitive edge. If we are to succeed in the

21st century, we need to Americanize America's schools. We need to do what we do best—educate all students, provide for high-quality basics, and simultaneously allow our students to explore, experiment, create, and develop as individuals.

Teacher Effectiveness in the United States and China

During the past decade, there has been a growing interest in better understanding what constitutes teacher effectiveness. This focus has presented both challenges and opportunities for policymakers, researchers, and practitioners to develop improvements in teacher preparation, recruitment, development, and evaluation. For instance, in the United States, where the tone of educational reform is leaning more and more toward accountability—with the Race to the Top initiative and the Elementary and Secondary Education Act (ESEA) Flexibility Plan—states are mandated to develop a teacher evaluation system that is rigorous in measuring teacher effectiveness, as indicated by student academic growth. In addition, abundant research has been conducted to examine the impact that movements toward standardization, accountability, and high-stakes assessment systems have had on teachers' practices, beliefs, attitudes, and overall effectiveness (e.g., Hamilton & Stecher, 2004; National Board on Educational Testing and Public Policy, 2003; Parke, Lane, & Stone, 2006).

In China, educators and researchers are beginning to reconceptualize teacher effectiveness in ways that will fulfill the ambitions of the national curriculum reform—particularly teachers' capacities to incorporate new curriculum standards and new approaches to thinking about student learning and teaching (e.g., Bo, 2008; Du, 2004; Sun, 2004; Wang, 2006; Zhang, 2008). Although studies regarding teacher effectiveness in the United States abound, "a limited number of empirical studies have been conducted in China" (Liu & Meng, 2008, p. 2). Against this backdrop of educational reform in the United States and China, and along with intensified global economic and educational competition, this is an opportune time to conduct an international comparative examination that sheds new light on and shares new perspectives about the complex issue of teacher effectiveness (Crossley & Waston, 2003).

Chinese educational reforms at national, provincial, and local levels are attempting to decrease the density of curriculum, encourage teachers to adopt more student-centered inquiry and problem-solving activities, empower teachers with more autonomy, and encourage teachers to be more innovative and flexible about the curriculum to better meet the needs of the students. By contrast, reform in the United States is driving its educational system toward centralization of elementary and secondary education. It is increasingly more test-oriented. Fang and Gopinathan (2009) note that educational reformers in the West are oriented toward better-structured subject content, as demonstrated in the Common Core State Standards, whereas the East is looking at how to involve students more actively in learning and how to relate learning to real applications.

These opposite trends of educational reform policies and practices highlight the fact that the Chinese and U.S. educational systems can be a potent source of learning for each other. Different countries can come together to explore best practices and "the problems others face, the objectives they seek, the routes they try, the results they arrive at, and the unintended results they produce are worth analysis" (Schwille, Dembele, & Schubert, 2007, p. 10).

Purpose of This Book

The purpose of this book is to shed light on the beliefs and practices of highly effective teachers in China (East) and the United States (West). In *West Meets East* we focus on what teachers in the East can learn from their counterparts in the West and vice versa. Of course, distinctive teaching cultures are formed and nurtured in specific educational systems (Stigler & Hiebert, 1999). Teaching practice, as a cultural action, occurs in specific cultural settings and evolves in ways that can reflect the underlying cultural values advocated and nurtured by the wider society (Leung, 1995; Li & Shimizu, 2009). The United States and China—two nations that are drastically different in demographics, history, political systems, and socioeconomic status—also differ dramatically in teaching systems and instructional practices. With that in mind, we set out to answer a few questions, not least of which were: Which beliefs and practices of effective teachers cross the cultural divide? Which are unique to each culture?

Compared with the abundance of research done in the United States, the field of teacher effectiveness is still largely uncharted in China—although it is gaining increasing attention. Earlier studies found that a salient feature of classrooms in cultures with a strong history of Confucian ethics is the dominance and directiveness of teachers in the teaching and learning process (e.g., Hiebert et al., 2003; Huang & Leung, 2004). However, whole-class direct instruction (i.e., lecturing) is not typically associated with teacher effectiveness in U.S. studies. The act of lecturing is often criticized in the West for the assumption that students are passive receivers in the process of learning and for an emphasis on learning at lower cognitive levels. Nevertheless, contrary to these beliefs, high-quality teaching and learning and active student engagement can still occur in strict, teacher-controlled classrooms, even when the class size is large (Hiebert et al., 2003; Huang & Leung, 2004).

This book is based on the fundamental premise that strong teaching by talented teachers is at the heart of educational quality, and that understanding the elements of good teaching requires a thorough exploration of both the practices and the professional thinking of exemplary teachers. Specifically, *West Meets East* comprises cross-case analyses of teachers in the United States and China who have won national awards for their teaching. These findings were generated from interviews with and observations of the teachers, using a number of standardized data-collection protocols and focusing on the teachers' beliefs about and patterns of teaching in their respective classrooms.

Background and Context

This study began as a collaboration among coauthors James Stronge, Catherine Little, and Leslie Grant, and it focused on award-winning teachers in the United States. Pat Popp joined the study later and brought with her a focus on award-winning teachers in the United States who work with at-risk and highly mobile students. We had the great fortune to work with Yaling Sun, a visiting scholar from China. Through a common interest in what constitutes teacher effectiveness, we launched a cross-cultural study of the beliefs and practices of award-winning teachers in the United States and China. Xianxuan Xu then joined the study as a graduate student at the time the study was conducted.

We used Stronge's (2007) framework of teacher quality as a basis for thinking about effective teaching and then developed this framework with additional concepts that were developed in parallel by Chinese researchers (e.g., Bai, 2000; Cui & Wang, 2005). By synthesizing these findings on teacher effectiveness, key qualities and behaviors of effective teachers emerged. The original framework includes six domains, as represented in Figure 1.2.

Several Chinese scholars explored the concept of teacher effectiveness and developed corresponding theoretical frameworks, but most of those efforts were based on conventional wisdom rather than on evidence generated by empirical studies (Cui, 2001; Cui & Wang, 2005; Sun, 2004). Nonetheless, the framework proposed by Cui and Wang (2005) is also composed of six major domains, and there is substantial overlap with Stronge's framework:

1. Developing an environment that is conductive to learning.
2. Studying and understanding students.
3. Clarifying goals and organizing learning content.
4. Providing varied learning opportunities.
5. Helping students learn how to learn.
6. Continuous reflection and innovation on instruction.

FIGURE 1.2   Qualities of Effective Teachers

---

1. *Prerequisites for Effective Teaching,* including characteristics such as a teacher's educational background, professional preparation, verbal ability, content knowledge, educational coursework, and teacher certification.
2. *Teacher as a Person,* with an emphasis on a teacher's nonacademic interactions with students and professional attitude.
3. *Classroom Management,* with the purpose of establishing a classroom environment that is conducive to teaching and learning.
4. *Planning for Instruction,* including the practices of maximizing the amount of time allocated for instruction, communicating expectations for student achievement, and planning for instructional purposes.
5. *Implementing Instruction,* including the practices of using instructional strategies according to particulars of student needs, understanding the complexities of teaching, using questioning techniques and supporting student engagement.
6. *Assessing Student Progress,* such as using homework and ongoing assessment to solicit data of student learning, providing meaningful feedback, and applying the findings of student learning outcomes to improve instruction.

Figure 1.3 provides an overview of the similarities among selected reviews of effective teacher beliefs and practices in both the United States and China.

The Teachers

As discussed earlier, this book involves a comparative analysis of national award-wining American and Chinese teachers. In order to examine individual teachers' practices and beliefs in depth, we drew a small—but diverse— sample of effective teachers. Given this focus, the participants should satisfy a level of scrutiny to be considered representative of excellent teaching in their respective countries. A substantial limitation of identifying excellent teachers was, first, how to define excellence and, second, how to find excellent teachers. In defining excellence, we were guided by Stronge's framework (2007), along with Chinese researchers' criteria mentioned earlier (Bai, 2000; Cui & Wang, 2005). We chose national award-winning teachers as the operational definition of excellence. Thus, teachers were invited to participate in the research study based on having received a teaching award from a national organization granting recognition across content areas and grade levels.

Accepting national award-winning teachers as excellent teachers is not a proof-perfect process. It is entirely possible that some teachers received awards for reasons other than exhibiting the qualifying criteria of excellence that we have adopted. There is no doubt that many deserving, truly outstanding teachers were overlooked in the various award selection processes. Nonetheless, absent a more perfect method for identifying teacher excellence (e.g., teacher effectiveness indices as measured by teachers' effects on student academic growth), the research team chose to accept the risk of equating national teacher awards with teacher excellence. In defense of this assumption, all awards that were considered, in both the United States and China, have a rigorous vetting process for identifying and determining their award winners. The U.S. awards considered in this study included the Milken Educator Award and Disney's American Teacher Award, along with induction into the National Teachers Hall of Fame. The Chinese award used was the National Teacher Excellence Award (全国优秀教师), which is bestowed by the Ministry of Education. In

Stronge, 2007	Danielson, 2007	Bai, 2000	Cui & Wang, 2005	Sun, 2004
Prerequisites of Effective Teaching	Planning and Preparation			
Teacher as a Person	Professional Responsibilities Classroom Environment	Reflective Practitioner	Study and Understand Students; Continuous Reflection and Innovation on Instruction	
Classroom Management	Classroom Environment	Classroom Management and Student Engagement	Learning Environment	Classroom Observation and Management
Planning for Instruction	Planning and Preparation	Instructional Planning	Clarify Intended Learning Outcomes and Organize Learning Content	Objectives of Teaching and Learning
Implementing Instruction	Instruction	Effective Instruction Models and Teacher-Student Interactions	Learning Opportunities	Learning Activities and Instructional Delivery
Monitoring Student Progress and Potential	Planning and Preparing Instruction	Feedback and Review		Monitoring of Both Learning and Teaching

both nations, reviews of these major national awards and achievements revealed that their criteria included some or all of the following qualities:

1. Contributions to education.
2. Recognition by the community and use of community resources.
3. Being a role model for students and other teachers.
4. Innovation in education.
5. Professionalism.
6. Excellent teaching practices.

Among these criteria, contributions to education and excellent teaching practices were most commonly cited. Recipients of awards highlighting these criteria were chosen to participate.

To illustrate, the Milken Educator Award, given in the United States, identifies and selects outstanding elementary and secondary school teachers "as evidenced by effective instructional practices and student learning results in the classroom and school" or as evidenced by "accomplishments beyond the classroom that provide models of excellence for the profession" (Milken Family Foundation, n.d.). In China, the National Teacher Excellence Award emphasizes the exceptional roles played by teachers as they inspire the development of their students as whole people. This award also recognizes teachers for exploring innovative instructional strategies that have a positive impact on their classroom effectiveness and students' learning outcomes (Ministry of Education of the People's Republic of China, n.d.).

In addition, we purposefully selected teachers who vary widely in their years of teaching experience, levels of teaching (e.g., elementary, secondary), content areas, geographic regions (e.g., urban, rural), and gender. In this study, this variation serves two purposes: to document the range of variation in the selected award-winning teachers and to determine whether common themes or patterns cut across this variation. Such patterns can take on added importance because they emerge out of great heterogeneity.

A total of 16 award-winning teachers from China and 15 from the United Stated were observed teaching and were interviewed about their beliefs and practices. Among the Chinese teachers, ten were female and six were male. Among the U.S. teachers, three were male, and twelve were female. All of the participants had more than five years of teaching experience, and

24 (15 from China and 9 from the United States) had more than ten years of experience. Among the Chinese teachers, five taught math, four taught science, and seven taught Chinese (Mandarin) language. The U.S. participants consisted of five math teachers, two science teachers, five English teachers, one music teacher, and two social studies teachers. Eight Chinese teachers taught at elementary schools, and eight taught at secondary schools. Nine U.S. teachers taught elementary grades, and six taught at the secondary level. These 31 teachers came from 31 different school districts, which were located in different geographic areas. For the Chinese teachers, four taught in suburban schools, four were from rural schools, and eight were from urban schools. Seven U.S. teachers taught in suburban schools, three were from rural schools, and five were from urban schools.

Multiple types of data were generated and collected. We visited each teacher for a day and observed at least one hour of formal instruction (and frequently more), interviewed each teacher using an interview protocol, and reviewed selected teaching artifacts (e.g., lesson plans, student work, handouts, blackboard/computer displays). By including multiple data sources, our intent was to provide a multidimensional understanding of the teachers teaching and working within their authentic natural teaching environments.

We used the Differentiated Classroom Observation Scale (Cassady et al., 2004) to collect information about teaching practices. Using the scale, we were able to gather data about the instructional strategies that were employed, the percentage of students who were engaged, who was responsible for directing the activities (i.e., teacher- versus student-directed), and the levels of cognitive demand that were required. In addition to the information gleaned from our direct observations, we kept field notes to document contextual information and specific aspects of teachers' behaviors that were not captured by the formal observation form. Although our field notes were not used as a primary data source, they were important in complementing the standardized observations and providing a more complete and credible representation of what was happening in the classrooms.

Structure of the Book

The chapters that follow present evidence of the qualities of effective teachers that were observed and documented in practice across multiple teaching contexts and across two quite different educational cultures. As noted earlier, the qualities that we focused on and used to organize the chapters include the teacher as a person, instructional planning, instructional delivery, and the learning environment. Our intent is to develop a richer understanding of teacher effectiveness through cross-cultural case studies that highlight the practices and beliefs of selected award-winning teachers in both the United States and China. Specifically, the chapters focus on several main themes related to teaching and learning:

- Chapter 2 focuses on teachers' personal qualities and relationships with students.
- Chapter 3 explores the instructional planning processes and the critical role of assessment in this process.
- Chapter 4 uncovers the instructional practices of award-winning teachers and reveals the instructional strategies that are used most often, the cognitive levels of instruction that are most prevalent, and teachers' views on effective instructional strategies.
- Chapter 5 examines classroom management styles and techniques and how they align with student engagement.
- Chapter 6 summarizes and provides implications for teaching in the United States and China. These implications are explored through a comparison of metaphors for teaching, as generated by the award-winning teachers.

In addition to examining similarities and differences in teaching and learning processes, Chapters 2–5 provide practical tools for consideration that are based on our observations and findings about effective teaching practices in both the United States and China.

Summary

In *West Meets East,* we have sought to get inside the so-called black box of education in both the United States and the People's Republic of China. The United States looks east to China and is captivated by the high scores on international assessments students in that country achieve. By contrast, China looks west and is enamored with how the United States fosters innovation and creativity in students.

Although the cultural contexts and educational systems certainly play a role in the differences between these countries' educational outcomes, the fact of the matter is that teachers are the ones, in both countries, who directly impact student learning. How do they do it? What lessons can teachers in the "West" learn from their colleagues in the "East," and vice versa? As the world continues to get flatter, our natural curiosity takes over and our ability to answer these questions can be realized. We trust that the findings presented in the following chapters will contribute to a richer understanding of a vital issue faced by both countries: teacher effectiveness.

2

The Teacher, The Person
第二章：教师作为个人

> *The close relationship with students definitely helps my classroom ins-*
> *truction. Just like what Confucius has proposed—"亲其师，信其道"—*
> *when the students trust the teacher/master, they will follow his way*
> *and trust the things that he teaches. —Chinese teacher*

> *It's my personal mindset that I've been given a year with these kids,*
> *and it's my responsibility to make sure that they grow that year, that*
> *they leave smarter and still excited about school. —U.S. teacher*

What do you remember most about your favorite teachers? The instructional strategies they used or the types of tests they gave? More than likely, when you remember your favorite teachers, you remember their personal qualities, how much they cared about you, their excitement for learning, and how they challenged you to learn. In China and the United States—just as it is in every country—it's the teacher who plays a central role in student learning. In the Confucian tradition,

Teachers are helpers who try to find out the unique character
of each of their students and guide him or her to accomplish

the golden mean, which harmonizes the poles of character—the excesses and the defects—and thus enables a learner to grow up to become a man of character. (Shim, 2008, p. 524)

In the U.S. tradition, the teacher plays a similar role. Speaking about a teacher's impact on students, John Dewey stated that "the teacher should be occupied not with subject matter in itself but in its interaction with the pupils' present needs and capacities. Hence 'simple scholarship is not enough' " (Dewey, 1916, p. 191). Dewey was speaking about the critical importance of pedagogy, but a clear implication of his work is that a teacher's personal qualities are paramount. Those qualities—qualities that we know almost intuitively but that are difficult to measure—are the ones that make teachers effective in helping students grow and learn.

Our work revealed four main themes about the personal qualities that make effective teachers in China and the United States. These include the following:

1. Fostering and maintaining *positive, productive relationships* with students and parents.
2. Having a *sense of purpose* and *responsibility* that extends beyond the day-to-day learning in the classroom.
3. Engaging in *professional development* over the course of a career.
4. Engaging in *self-reflection* to improve teaching and learning.

Although these themes emerged as commonalities among all of the teachers in our study, nuanced differences in teachers' approaches to these themes provide a window into cultural differences that can be instructive for educators in both countries.

———————— 教室聚光灯 ————————

CLASSROOM SPOTLIGHT

A 3rd grade teacher in the United States emphasized his relationships with students as the centerpiece of his teaching. His comments focused extensively on his efforts to acknowledge and respond to individual student needs and interests, and his students demonstrated their engagement and confidence as they took responsibility and showed initiative for their learning during a science experiment we observed. The positive relationships he had with students were also evident in the number of students who greeted him in the hallways and stopped by his classroom during breaks in the day. The teacher emphasized his perspective on education as a collaborative endeavor that relies on strong partnerships with parents. To that end, he made home visits early in the year, sitting around the kitchen table with parents—"on their turf"—to discuss shared goals for student progress.

Lesson 1: Build Positive, Productive Relationships

The importance of positive relationships with students and parents cannot be overstated. In the literature related to effective teaching (in any country or culture), the central role that positive, caring relationships play in student success is an overwhelmingly common theme. To illustrate, a meta-analysis of studies focusing on student-teacher relationships found that positive relationships are associated with positive outcomes, such as higher student engagement and academic achievement. Conversely, negative relationships between teachers and students affect these outcomes negatively (Roorda, Koomen, Spilt, & Oort, 2011). In addition, when parents, teachers, and students in both the United States and China are asked what makes an effective teacher, the responses cross cultural boundaries—teachers' close and personal relationships with students and parents is paramount (Liu & Meng, 2009; Stronge, 2007). Our work revealed that effective teachers in both countries view their relationships with students as vital and instrumental to their own success as teachers and, thus, to the success of their students. The following points are illustrative of the ways that teachers portrayed their relationships with their students:

- They establish a warm, friendly, trusting, and caring relationship with each student. They also demonstrate their care—either for academic or nonacademic aspects of students' growth—in ways that their students are aware.
- They get to know each student on a personal level. They also highlight developing relationships and connecting with students on an emotional or personal level.

- They view relationships as a conduit for student success in the classroom. They also understand that teacher-student relationships are important in achieving desired results with students, inspiring students to engage with the learning process, and encouraging students to behave appropriately in school.

─────────────── 教师的想法 ───────────────

TEACHERS' THOUGHTS ON RELATIONSHIPS

China / 中国

"I feel such a bond with them because I have them for so long. . . . Having them three years, by that point you get so close to them that you feel like if they do something wrong, it's out of their character in the relationship with you."

───●───

"When the students recognize you as a person, they will pay attention to the academic learning in your classroom and put in effort to learn your subject."

───●───

"When students like the teacher, they will like your classroom; and when they like your classroom, they will like the subject you teach."

───●───

"Just as a Chinese old saying says, I am a teacher and a friend at the same time. That describes my relationships with my students really well. I think that can help our relationships become more harmonious. A teacher should not be someone sitting high above and detached."

United States / 美国

"I try to have meaningful connections with them. You know, I try to know them as people and to meet their individual needs and have an understanding of what's going on at home."

───●───

"I think where I've been successful in the classroom is that just about every single student in there knows that I like them. They know it and I always try to find something important about them and I try to personalize them."

———•———

"I think knowing your students and making sure that they know that you care about them goes a thousand percent to getting results from them."

———•———

"I think that we have a deep sense of trust. My kids know that I believe in them and so they're willing to take risks."

These award-winning teachers regard the ethic of care and respect as a vital foundation for students' best learning and as a prerequisite for effective teaching. They are able to find a balance among respect for students as human beings, for student individuality, for discipline, and for academic success. Many teachers mentioned that they help their students with schoolwork, and many Chinese and U.S. teachers mentioned that they stayed in the classroom after school to provide one-on-one tutoring for students at risk of failing. In addition, they go the extra mile to help students with their personal problems and provide guidance. Figure 2.1 provides some tips for building positive relationships.

Lessons from the East

Although teachers in both countries view their relationships as critical to student success and to their roles as teachers, nuanced differences are instructive and indicative of the culture in which these teachers live and work. Teachers in China had more personal and family-like relationships with their students, and they often spoke of maintaining harmonious relationships. They also tended to project family relationships on their relationships with students by referring to relationships with students in terms of sister/brother or parent/child. Furthermore, they emphasized their responsibility of being a role model of moral perfection.

Such beliefs about moral guidance and parental roles might explain the vast majority of Chinese teachers' authoritarian and teacher-dominated instructional style. Indeed, research has pointed out that some distinguishing

FIGURE 2.1	Practical Tips for Building Relationships

1.	Administer interest surveys to get to know individual students. Use this information to spark conversations with students and incorporate students' interests into your lessons and other classroom materials.
2.	Use students' names often. Greet students as they enter the classroom by using their names. Teachers comment how this simple gesture goes a long way in demonstrating that they care about students, know them individually, and are glad they came to school.
3.	Provide opportunities for one-to-one conversations, such as lunchtime talks and after-school help sessions.
4.	Have fun with students. Even in classrooms with 40–50 students, teachers in China had a passion and drive for engaging students and making learning active and fun. Similarly, teachers in the United States were not afraid to joke around and did so in a way that supported—rather than detracted from—the learning process.
5.	Welcome family members into the school and classroom by communicating opportunities to volunteer their time and effort, eat lunch with their children, and have open and frank conversations with you.
6.	Begin communication home to students' families early, before the school year even begins. Build a community within the classroom and with family members.

traits of Chinese culture promote a certain amount of overlap between school/classroom and family—children are expected to be submissive to their parents, there is strong interdependence among family members, and children are raised with the belief that their school performance reflects on their family's honor (Blair & Qian, 1998). The following quotes are most illuminating:

"First of all, as a teacher, you have to care about and love the students, just like their parents."

———•———

"When you have your students in your heart, you will treat them like the children in your own family."

———•———

"Sometimes, some students would call me 'Mom,' and I say, 'I am your mom. While you are at school, I am your mom.' "

———————●———————

"The relationship between me and my students can be described as a relationship between siblings."

Lessons from the West

The relationships between the U.S. teachers and students, by contrast, were more professional and community-based. Teachers spoke of caring for their students but in a way that is subtly distinct from their Chinese counterparts. Teachers in the United States are more likely to focus on caring within the context of a professional teacher-student relationship. The following quotes illustrate this approach:

"I just try to know them as people and try to meet them each day where they are. And also know their interests, so that I can make my lessons meaningful to them."

———————●———————

"They understand that I'm their teacher and that they're my students, but that's not how we function. I'm more of a facilitator and they're the drivers of the learning."

———————●———————

"They know that I love them and that I care about them and want them to enjoy learning."

The teachers who highlighted relationships with students most thoroughly were also the ones who made the most comments about relationships with parents. This was not a coincidence. One teacher mentioned the necessity of strong home-school connections and of understanding what is happening at home. Another teacher, in particular, spoke extensively about working in partnership with parents from an initial meeting to ongoing discussions throughout the year:

"Once you get that base developed of a relationship with a parent, you're not as hesitant, you're not as afraid, you're not concerned about calling them up and saying, 'Look, you know what your child did today? And, how are we going to help him not do that again?' . . . I'm not afraid to do that. Because they know what my intent is. And when you've not had conversations, and you've not developed a relationship with parents, they don't know where you're coming from."

Teachers spoke of their relationships with parents and with their students beyond the classroom with a broad sense of the larger community. One teacher commented, "My relationship with the child is community-based. It's not just 'I'm teaching you between 9:00 and 3:00, but it's my whole life, because that's my vocation.'" Earlier research found that Western teachers (including U.S. teachers) tend to view their involvement in students' learning within the framework of professional responsibilities as defined by the job description, whereas teachers in China may go beyond their professional duties to become personally involved with their students' learning (Ho, 2001).

Lesson Tool:
Student Interest Survey

Effective teachers know that establishing positive relationships with students at the beginning of the school year should be a top priority. Read almost any text on classroom management and you'll find a section devoted to this topic (e.g., Jones & Jones, 2012; Scott, Anderson, & Alter, 2011). In this section, we've provided some tips for building relationships, but there are also many tools that can help in that process, particularly at the beginning of the year. One such tool is a student interest survey. Though teachers are obviously talking to their students as a means to building relationships, a quick student survey can go a long way in that process. Simply asking students about their interests and hobbies is an indication that the teacher cares about them as people. In addition, this information can be used to spark conversations or plan high-interest lessons.

One example we saw in China involved students finding the hypotenuse of a triangle that formed from a shadow on a basketball court. Many students in this class enjoyed basketball, and the teacher knew it. Therefore, the teacher fashioned his academic example around student interest. Similarly, a teacher in the United States used sports statistics as a way to teach statistics with her students who were interested in sports. Figure 2.2

FIGURE 2.2	Student Interest Survey

Name: _____

I am excited about our work together this year and would like to get to know some things about you. Please answer the following questions to the best of your ability. You may skip any questions that you do not wish to answer.

1. What is the last good book you read?

2. What made the book good?

3. What is the last good movie you saw?

4. What made the movie good?

5. What type of music do you like?

6. What sports do you like to watch and/or play?

7. To what clubs do you belong?

8. When you get home from school, what's the first thing you do?

9. If you could eat anything for dinner tonight, what would you like to eat?

10. How would you describe yourself as a friend?

11. How would you describe your best friend?

12. Whom do you most admire? Why?

13. What is your favorite thing to do?

14. What animal would best describe your personality? Why?

provides an example of such a survey. Any survey would need to be crafted for the specific grade level and context within which it would be used.

——— 教室聚光灯 ———

CLASSROOM SPOTLIGHT

A 1st grade teacher in China with 46 students (yes, 46 students!) taught a lesson on the use of Chinese language. As part of the lesson, students brought 5 yuan (about $1) and were taken on a field trip to the corner market. (Just imagine: 46 1st graders—with money—on a field trip to the corner market!) The point of the lesson was to learn vocabulary associated with shopping. However, when we interviewed the teacher, she indicated that another point of the lesson was to develop moral character. After the field trip, she asked her students whether they bought something for themselves or for their mother, father, or grandparent. She rounded out the lesson by talking about how it is important to think of other people and not just their own wants.

Lesson 2: Foster a Sense of Purpose and Responsibility

In reflecting upon their teaching practices, teachers in both the United States and China felt a sense of responsibility for their students' success and a sense of purpose in their work beyond the day-to-day objectives of teaching. None of our interview questions directly asked teachers to explain their motivations for teaching or their sense of purpose, yet these themes emerged time and again among all teachers:

• **Educating the whole child.** Teachers in both China and the United States commented that their purpose is not only to teach knowledge but also to educate students as a whole person. Teachers in both countries focused on academics but often spoke of the unwritten or tacit curriculum—the social and moral development of children.

- **Serving as role models.** Teachers in both countries saw their primary responsibility to be teaching content knowledge, but they also sought to serve as role models in academic and moral development.

- **Being aware of the larger educational system and its impact on students.** Teachers demonstrated an awareness of the larger systems in which they work, including the school, school district, and profession, as well as larger societal systems. This awareness can be classified into three primary areas of emphasis: (1) influence of external expectations and recommendations on their work, (2) recognition of how the larger environment influences students' lives, and (3) concern for the quality of their profession.

--------- 教师的想法 ---------

TEACHERS' THOUGHTS ON
SENSE OF PURPOSE AND RESPONSIBILITY

China / 中国

"The responsibilities of a teacher are not only to transmit the knowledge of subject matter but also to nourish the students as a whole person."

———•———

"During the first year of my teaching career, I was the mentor teacher of only one class. Since then, I have become the leading teacher of two or three classes. How could that happen? (Why did parents, students, and the principal have so much trust in me?) Because I have a sense of responsibility and commitment."

United States / 美国

"It's not just about the content and the curriculum. It's about them [the students] as a whole person, and we want what is absolutely best for every single child that's in here."

———•———

"[I would like to influence students in] the kinds of things that don't have anything to do with the content but have to do with the idea that learning can be joyful, that learning makes us human and gives us tools to be real people and enjoy our lives."

———•———

"[I want to continue] to present a positive face, persona, [and] picture to the community, so the people in [my state] continue to have a great deal of respect in public education. And that the kids that we are educating today across the United States will help us to continue to be leaders in democracy in the 21st century."

Lessons from the East

The focus on testing in China and the high-stakes nature of national examinations results weighs heavily on the minds of Chinese students and teachers alike. Indeed, when parents and students have been asked about qualities that make an effective teacher, strong test performance is one of them (Liu & Meng, 2009). It's not surprising that test scores form an integral part of a teacher's evaluation (Liu & Teddlie, 2004). Teachers typically feel a sense of responsibility toward an entire family, since China's one-child policy usually has meant that each student is his or her family's one opportunity for upward mobility. The following quotes not only illuminate this sense of purpose and responsibility but also demonstrate how award-winning teachers in China view themselves as role models to students:

> "Because I am the head teacher, I spend a lot of time with my students after class, and I monitor their moral development. I think it's important for these teenagers to have moral guidance. They spend most of their time in this school and in this classroom, so it's of great significance for me to be a role model."

———•———

> "We are trying very hard to be effective teachers. Because the current situation in China is each family has only one child (because of the one-child policy). The parents have great expectations for their children's education."

———•———

"Each teacher would have some stress; this is natural, because of the high expectations from the larger society."

Ban Zhu Ren
班主任

A *ban zhu ren* in China is the lead teacher for a class of children—in both their academic and moral development. In China, each class has a fixed classroom and ban zhu ren. The closest equivalent in the United States might be a home-room teacher or tutor who has been assigned to a specific group of children. However, the ban zhu ren's role is far broader in scope and responsibility. A ban zhu ren usually teaches one subject area but is also responsible for ensuring classroom discipline, organizing student involvement in school and community activities, meeting and advising parents, and working with other subject-matter teachers to solve classroom problems.

Lessons from the West

All of the U.S. teachers in our study referenced the influence of external forces on their teaching, including standards and assessments at the local, state, and national levels. Indeed, critics of the standards movement explain that standards and testing have led to more standardized teaching practices within the United States and less autonomy in the classroom (Au, 2011). In addition, teachers are impacted by the structures surrounding them since structure drives behavior (Senge et al., 2012). Studies over the past 20 years have examined reasons why U.S. teachers leave the teaching profession. One reason that continues to emerge is that of workplace conditions and administrative support at both the building and school district levels (Sedivy-Benton & McGill, 2012). In addition, teachers are concerned about the lack of respect and support for teaching as a profession (Ingersoll, 2007). However, we found that these award-winning teachers worked within the system, strove to elevate the profession, and maintained some degree of autonomy during an era of standardized curriculum and testing.

"My challenge is figuring out ways to make our profession better . . . making sure that our colleges are preparing kids to come into the field adequately."

———•———

"We need to connect and remember—get rid of the amnesia—why we became educators to begin with. And have enough courage to put that out in front."

Lesson Tool:
Teaching and Learning Philosophy Statement

Do you remember why you went into education in the first place? What do you believe is the role of the teacher in the classroom? What do you believe about how students learn? If you went through a traditional teacher preparation program in the United States, then you most likely developed a philosophy of teaching and learning that has evolved over time. Likewise, if you are a teacher in China, then your philosophy has also likely developed and been molded over time. A strong connection between great teachers in both the United States and China is that they have a strong sense of purpose. They know what they believe about their own teaching, about student learning, and how the two interact.

Writing a teaching and learning philosophy statement can be a cathartic experience that helps a teacher recapture his or her sense of purpose. Many teachers who have developed such a philosophy post it on their personal or class website or share portions of it in classroom newsletters. Here are some questions to guide you as you write your own philosophy of teaching and learning:

1. What do you believe about the role of the teacher in student learning and development?
2. What do you believe about the relationships between student and teacher?
3. How would you describe the classroom environment and its impact on teaching and learning?
4. How do students learn best?
5. How do you evaluate the success of your teaching?
6. If you could provide a metaphor for teaching and learning, what would it be?

These six simple questions illuminate one very complex question: What do you believe about teaching and learning? By developing a philosophy statement, you have the rare opportunity to reclaim and rekindle your sense of purpose.

Lesson 3: Engage in Sustained, Lifelong Professional Development

When reflecting on their growth as professionals, teachers from the United States and China remarked that they learned from their daily practices as a site for inquiry, much like action research in the classroom. Their professional development evolved over time, with teachers from both countries recognizing that they are different teachers as veterans than they were as novices. Some Chinese teachers also shared how their country's national curriculum reform disrupted their long-held beliefs regarding teaching and learning. Nevertheless, they rose up to the challenge and rode the wave of external reforms. Their professional growth was an ongoing process of experimenting with new strategies, studying the effects, and then generating new approaches to extend their repertoire of instructional experiences. Such self-initiated and autonomic growth required observation and reflection, and it required the skill to persevere, seek evidence, take risks, and remain open-minded to change (Feiman-Nemser, 2001).

The following section details key aspects of professional growth and development:

- **Engagement in the broader educational community:** These award-winning teachers were all involved with various forms of professional development activities, such as mentoring, peer coaching, supervising practicing teachers or interns, attending conferences or workshops, pursuing coursework toward an advanced degree, or serving in professional organizations.
- **Influence of colleagues:** Award-winning teachers in the United States and China understand the importance of having trusted colleagues with whom they can discuss ideas, provide support, and learn together as teachers.
- **Emergence as a leader:** These teachers were involved in professional development activities beyond the walls of their classrooms. Teachers in the

United States worked at the district level to secure grants for funding projects, writing curriculum, and serving on district-level committees. Chinese teachers served as demonstration teachers and led professional development initiatives at their schools and beyond. In addition, the Chinese teachers were prolific scholars and researchers in their subject areas and were well-known in their respective fields. Some of them even gave presentations and demonstration lessons around the nation; U.S. teachers also presented at state and national conferences.

教师的想法

TEACHERS' THOUGHTS ON PROFESSIONAL DEVELOPMENT

China / 中国

"Professional development is a multifold process. The teachers have to be learners themselves."

———•———

"I think one influential experience is the teacher continuing education. Because I only have a two-year college degree, I need to invest a lot time in learning."

———•———

"I have participated twice in the Beijing 'backbone teachers' seminars [a professional development program for teacher leaders, who are often responsible for overseeing the instructional quality of certain subjects or grade levels in their schools], which were organized by the Beijing Institute of Education."

United States / 美国

"I never pass up an opportunity to go look at another teacher, to go be in another teacher's classroom, because having a window into another teacher's classroom . . . I always have something to learn."

Lessons from the East

The strongest lesson gleaned from teachers in China is the focus on collaboration and peer review of lessons. Though some U.S. teachers talked about the value of being in other teachers' classrooms, it was not as pervasive a technique for professional growth and change as in China. We found one striking difference between teachers in China and the United States: the former improve their teaching through "lesson research" (*kēyán* 科研)— cycles of activities in which teachers are grouped by subject and grade level to design, implement, and critique lessons together (Tsui & Wong, 2009). Another format of in-service professional development activity that teachers in China found helpful was "open lessons" (*gōngkāikè* 公开课), which are exemplary demonstration lessons given by expert teachers from within the local district, from a different area in the province, or from a different province altogether (Tsui & Wong, 2009).

Lesson Research
科研

Lesson research is an essential tool in the preparation, development, and continued growth of teachers in China (Kennedy & Lee, 2008). Observations are conducted in many ways to fit the needs of preservice or in-service teachers. The table below provides examples of some of the different types of lesson observations used.

shìfànkè 示范课 (demonstration lesson)	Experienced teachers teach a lesson to demonstrate a specific instructional strategy for novice teachers.
zhǐdǎokè 指导课 (supervised lesson)	Novice teachers conduct lessons that are supervised by expert teachers.
gōngkāikè 公开课 (open lesson)	Teachers teach lessons to colleagues to disseminate a specific approach or instructional strategy.

In China, teamwork is institutionalized, mostly in the form of school-level teacher research groups and grade-level lesson preparation groups (Fang & Gopinathan, 2009). Paine (1990) noted that these collaborative opportunities socialized teachers into "a community that shares a common body of knowledge and speaks a common language" (p. 75). One teacher commented,

> In this office, as you can see, the desks next to mine are owned by teachers who teach the same subject and grade level as me. Each Tuesday afternoon, we sit down together and talk with others about our teaching and our students' learning. What went well and didn't go well? We analyze our students' work and compare our students' progress over time. When we run into challenges, we consult others for problem-solving strategies. At the beginning of each semester, we study the curriculum and the textbook. We also share materials and give other emotional support.

Lessons from the West

Teachers in the United States commented on numerous ways that they continued their development as teachers. Key professional development experiences included the following:

- National Board Certification process: "It made me much more analytical and reflective about what I do."
- Coursework beyond initial teacher preparation: "There we really honed in on theory and the workings of a child and we got to begin to explore what makes a child tick, what kind of activities can you do."
- Opportunities to work as a demonstration teacher in a professional development institute and to attend annual conferences: "I could choose the sessions I needed at the time, and every year, as I got better at what I was doing or I knew what I wanted to learn, then I could sort of step up what I was choosing to something different, and so it was absolutely tailored to my needs."
- Self-study through readings: "Specifically, what really helped me out was Ruby Payne's framework for understanding poverty. That was helpful for me; it was a real a-ha that I am a middle-class person, and I am

not working with middle-class students, and they [and their parents] have a completely different framework than I do."

Lesson Tool:
Lesson Study

In our study of great teachers, we used a sampling technique called maximum variation sampling. We wanted maximum variation within both countries in terms of school level, geographic region, and subject matter. In both countries, we had teachers at all school levels teaching various subjects in urban, suburban, and rural settings. In China, we observed and interviewed teachers in the major political and economic hubs as well as teachers thousands of miles away in small towns. Through this maximum variation, a striking technique emerged across China—the use of lesson study. All 16 teachers mentioned this technique as key to their professional development. By contrast, only one U.S. teacher mentioned lesson study specifically.

This is not to say that lesson study does not occur in the United States; much has been written on the topic, and it has been used in schools (e.g., Hurd & Lewis, 2011; Stepanek, Appel, Leong, Mangan, & Mitchell, 2006). However, it is not a systematic approach that is used among teachers at all school levels and in all content areas. This is a key difference between the United States and China, where teachers would leave the doors to their classrooms open to one another as a tool for improvement. Although first implemented in Japan, this practice has clearly been embraced by teachers in China (Fang & Gopinathan, 2009; Stigler & Hiebert, 1999). Figure 2.3, which is based on the work of Lewis (2002), describes the steps to conducting a lesson study.

教室聚光灯

CLASSROOM SPOTLIGHT

Many of the Chinese teachers we observed opened their lessons with a quick review of what was learned in the previous lesson. During the few minutes of this brief review, they not only reviewed the strengths and weaknesses of student learning as demonstrated in the homework but also

FIGURE 2.3	Lesson Study Cycle

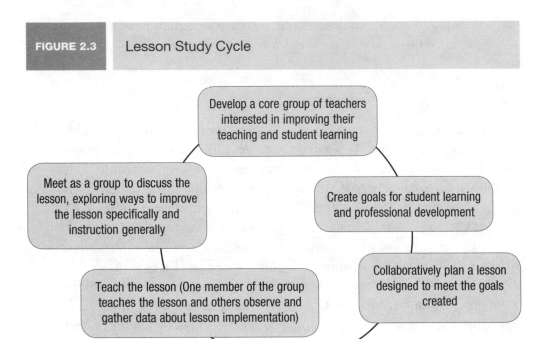

Source: From *Lesson Study: A Handbook of Teacher-Led Instructional Change,* by C. Lewis, 2002, Philadelphia: Research for Better Schools. Copyright 2002 by Research for Better Schools.

Resources for Engaging in Lesson Study

Lewis, C. (2002). *Lesson study: A handbook of teacher-led instructional change.* Philadelphia: Research for Better Schools.	This resource provides the specific tools and techniques for implementing lesson study, focusing not only on the essential steps but also on the supports needed to sustain the effort.
Stepanek, J., Appel, G., Leong, M., Mangan, M. T., & Mitchell, M. (2006). *Leading lesson study: A practical guide for teachers and facilitators.* Thousand Oaks, CA: Corwin.	This book breaks down the lesson study process and provides solid direction in implementing the process. In addition, sample research lessons are provided, along with helpful resources.

reflected on the weaknesses of their teaching. For instance, one teacher said, "I thought about the examples that I gave yesterday. I don't think they were very effective for the purpose of concept attainment, and I've thought up better ones." Another said, "Reflecting on the problem-solving process that I illustrated yesterday, and based on your homework, I think I didn't do a good job in presenting one of the steps. I will use just a few minutes to present it in a different manner and see if it works better." These teachers openly critiqued their teaching and promptly retaught or modified their instruction for better student learning.

Lesson 4: Practice Continual Self-Reflection

A common theme in the educational literature from both countries is that of a reflective practitioner (Bai, 2000; Cui & Wang, 2005; Stronge, 2007). We found strong evidence of self-reflection in award-winning U.S. and Chinese teachers with striking similarities in their engagement in self-reflection. Thus, these findings are presented jointly as lessons from the East and West. Although no questions in our interview specifically asked whether or how often teachers engaged in self-reflection, this practice emerged as one that teachers in both China and the United States found to be essential to professional growth and change. Teachers spoke of how they used reflection in their instructional planning and how they used feedback to grow as professionals.

Teachers systematically reflected on lessons taught. They used these reflections to inform further planning for the next day, the next unit, and the next year. A teacher in China commented,

> "During the first five years of teaching, I would have a self-reflection meeting just by myself every week, usually on Fridays. I would spend at least two hours to reflect on and critique the learning content I taught, the instructional methods I used, and the level of student achievement of learning objectives in the past week."

A U.S. teacher took a similar approach: "I step back and say, 'Am I going through this too slowly, or do I need to pick things up a little bit to still cover the things that are important, or is this really worth focusing on? Should I adjust my long-term plan?' "

Some teachers continually sought feedback from others for use in self-reflection. They commented on the value of self-evaluation and feedback and of their efforts to solicit feedback on their practice and use experiences with other teachers as a means of promoting self-evaluation. One U.S. teacher said that she found the videotaping and self-evaluation portion of the National Board Certification Process to be "one of the most exhilarating things I ever did. I loved it! I loved looking at what I was doing objectively and honestly." Similarly, a teacher in China stated that "we also delivered demonstration lessons in different schools, to be critiqued by other teachers and also to critique the lesson given by other teachers, and also to write reflexive journal [entries] on classroom practices afterward. This self-reflection was the most powerful component for me in improving my classroom practices."

Finally, many teachers used reflection for continual improvement and growth. They noted specific areas within their practice that they targeted for immediate or future improvement. In several cases, those areas for growth were personal habits and characteristics, such as organization, rather than pedagogical skills. In other cases, teachers highlighted teaching practices or content emphases for improvement, such as building more differentiation into questioning or improving wait time. One U.S. teacher described an effort he made over a period of several years to improve his reading instruction, developing and working toward specific goals, reading reference materials to support his work, and carefully evaluating his progress. He commented that he was working to make similar improvements to his mathematics teaching. "One of the good things about teaching is that you begin again every year. . . . Some years things just click and you go higher and higher, and other years you don't. But each year, one of the best things about teaching is that you begin again. . . . You get to reexamine what you did."

Many teachers in China said they kept a journal for the purpose of professional reflection. They commented in their journals on what worked in that day's teaching, such as interesting dialogues, beneficial examples, thought-provoking questions, fun hands-on activities, and effective technology. They also wrote down what did *not* work, such as unclear explanations or miscommunication that made them blind to the learning needs of some students. "My teaching methods are constantly changing. My ideology is constantly evolving as well. Alongside the national curriculum reform and educational research that has been done internationally, I am continuously improving and growing."

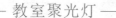

CLASSROOM SPOTLIGHT

A U.S. elementary school teacher was observed guiding students in a project that involved developing books about different animal species. The teacher noted to the observer that the lessons observed were different from lessons he had indicated (in advance) would be observed. He explained his thorough process of self-reflection and the balance between consistent long-term goals and individual lessons that were planned a day at a time. He talked about how he would reflect daily on where the class was, where it was headed, and what changes needed to be made, with a focus on how to adjust daily plans that progress toward long-term goals and how to recognize when those long-term goals might themselves need adjustment.

Lesson Tool:
Videotape and Self-Reflection

Teachers in both the United States and China talked about the use of peer observation as a means of self-reflection, but only U.S. teachers mentioned the practice of videotaping themselves teach as a method to improve teaching and learning in their classrooms. This approach involves videotaping a lesson, analyzing the implementation of the lesson, and then reflecting on that implementation—a similar approach to collaborative lesson study. Figure 2.4 provides an outline for analyzing and reflecting on a videotaped lesson.

Summary

Teacher preparation programs in China and the United States focus on building knowledge and skills in teaching (Ingersoll, 2007). However, the intangible qualities of an effective teacher are what seem to matter in both

FIGURE 2.4   Analysis and Reflection of a Videotaped Lesson

Use the following questions to guide your own analysis of and reflection on a lesson you have videotaped.

Description of the lesson

1. What was the main goal of the lesson? In other words, what should students know and be able to do by the end of the lesson?

2. What instructional strategies and resources/materials were chosen for the lesson, and why were they chosen?

3. What assessments were used during the lesson to check student understanding?

Analysis

4. What was one aspect of the lesson that was successful?

5. What was one aspect of the lesson that presented a challenge?

6. How do you know whether students learned what you intended for them to learn?

Reflection

7. If you were to teach this same lesson again, what would you keep the same and what would you change?

8. In general, what changes in instruction are you led to implement and why?

9. How would the change(s) impact student learning?

countries. If a teacher knows how to use a specific strategy but cannot develop and foster relationships with students, can students truly grow and develop? If a teacher is a subject-matter expert but fails to recognize the far-reaching aims of education, will students know why learning math, science, history, or language is important? If a teacher uses only the knowledge and skills learned in preservice preparation and does not engage in professional growth, can students then grow?

These are the intangibles—the personal qualities that cut across cultures and help define effective teaching. Although nuanced differences exist between countries, and we can learn from one another the tools and techniques for fostering relationships and engaging in professional development and self-reflection, the desire and passion to educate children and the willingness to change to meet students' needs is what makes award-winning teachers truly special—whether they teach in Shaanxi Province or Washington state.

In analyzing the interview transcripts, we identified words and phrases that were used repeatedly, by teachers in both countries, to describe personal qualities of teachers:

caring	关爱	humorous	幽默	trustworthy	可信任的
curious	好奇	love of learning	热爱学习	willing to take risks	敢于冒险
enthusiastic	感兴趣	passionate	热情的		

3

The Teacher, Instructional Planning, and Assessment

第三章：教师，备课和测试

Planning plays an important role in my instruction. I always think that one of the essential prerequisites of a successful lesson is a rigorous planning process. Planning, but plan what? That's a key question. First, you need to plan the curriculum, syllabus, and content that needs to be covered. And second, and this is crucial, is to plan the students—you need to have a deep understanding/ knowledge of your students to prepare a successful lesson. —Chinese teacher

Kieran Egan wrote a lot about story form in planning—a beginning, a middle, and an end. And I really always make sure that that's the case. And he also has this famous statement "why should it matter to children?" So I try to have the lessons be things that the kids would be invested in. And that's been a real challenge, because they really are different even from 3rd to 5th grade—what they want to be doing and what they care about. So every year I have to shift the units a little bit to get closer and closer to what they care about at that age level. —U.S. teacher

As anyone who has ever tried it knows, teaching is a complex process that involves careful preparation and planning, both for short-term and long-term learning purposes. Misulis (1997) commented that "regardless of the teaching model and methods used, effective instruction begins with careful, thorough, and organized planning on the part of the teacher" (p. 45). A solid planning process is integral to a teacher's efforts in identifying appropriate curriculum, instructional strategies, and resources to address the needs of all students. Furthermore, the extent of teachers' planning influences the content of instruction, the sequence and cognitive demands of subject topics, learning activities, students' opportunities to learn, and the pacing and allocation of instructional time.

Despite the central role that planning plays in teaching, it doesn't seem to come naturally to all teachers. In fact, it is abundantly clear that effective and less effective teachers plan differently. Some of these differences are reflected in the following research results. These studies are drawn predominantly from U.S.-based research; however, given the findings we obtained from our recent U.S.-China study, it seems safe to say that these attributes are also applicable to Chinese teachers.

- Facilitate planning units in advance to make intra- and interdisciplinary connections (McEwan, 2002).
- Construct a blueprint of how to address the curriculum during instructional time (McEwan, 2002).
- Develop well-organized and thoughtfully constructed lesson plans so they can become more effective leaders in the classroom and make more efficient use of class time (Panasuk, Stone, & Todd, 2002).
- Sequence material to promote students' cognitive and developmental growth (Panasuk et al., 2002).
- Plan for the different ability levels, backgrounds, and developmental needs of all students (Lucas, 2005).
- Use knowledge of available resources to determine what resources they need to acquire or develop (Buttram & Waters, 1997).
- Plan instruction in a multisourced manner (Allington & Johnston, 2000).

So why plan? Given the research noted above, along with a considerable number of other studies as evidence, one conclusion is clear (and rather self-evident): *effective teachers plan effectively.*

The U.S.-China project that serves as the backbone for this book revealed that award-winning teachers from both countries epitomize many of the previously mentioned attributes. In particular, we found six prominent themes relevant to how effective teachers plan—four with a high degree of similarity among teachers from the two countries and two that are distinctly different between teachers in China and the United States.

Lesson Similarities
1. Planning based on the *curriculum* and *students' learning needs.*
2. Incorporating *student assessments* in the planning process.
3. Allowing lessons to follow a *different path.*
4. Using *mental planning models.*

Lesson Differences
5. Using a *uniform planning structure.*
6. Engaging in *collaborative planning* or embracing *individual autonomy.*

In each of these themes—including those that are similar and those that are different—there are excellent lessons to be learned for all teachers. Each of these six themes will be explored, in turn, in the remainder of this chapter.

教室聚光灯

CLASSROOM SPOTLIGHT

A 3rd grade U.S. teacher was guiding his students to develop books about animal species, with guidelines open enough to allow students at varied levels of readiness to respond to the task. He specifically discussed his efforts toward this end: "I try to plan activities that different kids can access with success." To illustrate, he identified specific students and explained the differences in how each responded to the task while still engaged with the entire class toward the same general goal.

Lesson 1: Plan to the Curriculum and Students' Learning Needs

When we interviewed teachers, they spoke in detail about their approach to instructional planning. In fact, to a person, they noted the connectivity and relationship between curriculum and teaching and the vital role this connection made in their planning and actions. Interestingly, the specific needs of their students—that is, student assessments (a point made later in this chapter)—never strayed far from their thinking as they planned. All of the teachers in our study discussed aligning their instructional plans with the curriculum and individual students' learning needs in mind.

The teachers included in the study commented that they start their planning with an in-depth study of curriculum standards while keeping their planning relevant to students' needs. In addition, teachers in both countries agreed that effective student learning requires a progressive and coherent set of learning objectives. They often referred to district curricula and state/provincial, and national standards to identify the generic domains of subject content to be covered. Furthermore, they were aware that it was their responsibility to delineate the intended outcomes of each lesson and describe the behaviors or actions that students should be able to perform after participating in the learning activities.

For the three illustrations in the following section, note the explicit or implicit connectivity among curriculum, instructional delivery, and assessment of student learning. In the early stages of planning, these teachers recognized how essential it is to address the curriculum-instruction-assessment triad.

教师的想法

TEACHERS' THOUGHTS ABOUT THE RELATIONSHIPS AMONG CURRICULUM, INSTRUCTION, AND ASSESSMENT

China / 中国

"I will ask myself, 'What's the aim?,' 'What kind of goal do I want to get?,' and 'How can I get there?' I also ask myself questions like, 'What issues do I want to clarify? What problems will the students have? How do I organize the activities?' "

———————•———————

"High-quality planning is a prerequisite of a successful lesson. For me, planning means two levels of lesson preparation. The first is to analyze the curriculum and clarify what should be taught. Effective teaching requires that there is a progressive and coherent set of learning objectives. The second—even more important—is that planning is not just about the curriculum or the textbooks. It is about the students. Are they cognitively ready to learn new content? What are their interests? How do they learn best?"

United States / 美国

"First, I'd start with our curriculum, and I'd think of where the holes are. I've been changing a lot because I just started teaching [4th grade students] two years ago. And so I've really been honing it down to the topic areas we have outlined in our curriculum, and I look at it and I think, 'What's been missing?' So if I had to create a new unit, like the treasure hunt one we just finished, I'd say we need something on transportation and getting around. And then the next question I ask myself is, 'What's the assessment going to look like?' "

Lessons from the East and West

Given the unanimity of evidence from teachers in both countries, joint findings are described here (and in other sections beneath this heading). The dynamic interplay among curriculum, instruction, and assessment was a familiar theme expressed by the teachers. Figure 3.1 depicts the guiding framework for instructional planning as a triad of these elements.

The alignment of these components is essential to successful teaching and student learning. Teachers could use state or district curriculum standards, school district curriculum goals and objectives, and learning outcomes developed by professional organizations to plot the scope and sequence of subject topics. They also could apply their knowledge of

| FIGURE 3.1 | Key Elements of Instructional Planning |

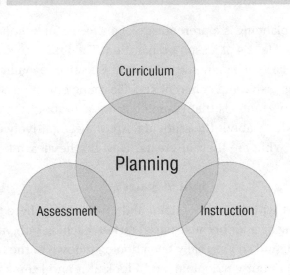

research-based practices to plan what strategies and techniques will be adopted to deliver instruction. Nevertheless, the most informative source for any form of instructional planning resides in teachers' classrooms: students. This is where assessment plays a role. Here, assessment is not only about how to evaluate student achievement but also, more importantly, about how to use assessment in pursuit of student success. In other words, in addition to assessment *of* learning, there should be assessment *for* learning. Incorporating assessment in planning can encourage teachers to monitor the adequacy of student learning, identify students in need of additional or different forms of instruction, and modify pedagogical strategies to maximize student learning.

Another key finding is that all of the teachers understood that integrating curriculum requirements with student needs requires a careful balancing act. They need to implement the curriculum faithfully while, simultaneously, addressing the unique learning needs of their students. In essence, this required them to stick to required curricular structures while exercising an appropriate degree of freedom and flexibility when it comes to their actual teaching. This balancing act was described aptly by one of the U.S. teachers:

> "I have rough ideas of where I'm going. . . . There are units that they would like for us to cover, like there's an architecture unit in 4th grade . . . but we have free reign of how we do that. They would like us to [include] bridges for 5th grade architecture, so my 5th graders are in the middle of building bridges right now. But other than that, it's pretty much up to us what we do. At the beginning of last year, I had a really hard time. People would say, 'Oh, the sky's the limit' and I'd say, 'Oh, the sky is really big, and where do we go?' "

A third key lesson related to the curriculum-instruction-assessment interplay is that teachers come to their classrooms with a multifaceted blueprint that often includes the following considerations:

- What to teach.
- How to teach it.
- How much time to take in teaching it.
- What materials and methods to use in teaching.
- What questions to ask.
- What unique learning needs their students have.
- How to assess whether their students actually learned the intended outcomes.

And the list goes on and on. Another way to state the obvious is that effective teachers never walk into a classroom with a blank slate. Rather, they come to their students with a rich, deep, detailed, differentiated, and often flexible plan to guide the connectivity among curriculum, teaching, assessment—and learning.

教室聚光灯

CLASSROOM SPOTLIGHT

A kindergarten teacher in the United States explained that after more than 20 years of experience, she had most of her lesson plans in her head.

However, she said that—particularly for sequences of related lessons—she kept folders with important bullet points about the lessons and with key assessment details indicating student progress. For a coin-counting lesson on the day of our visit, she showed us her preassessment data from the day before and how she intended to group and provide differentiated instruction for students based on their prior knowledge of basic skills in counting money. She also described her spur-of-the-moment decision to allow students to act out a book about pennies, based on their engagement with the book and the opportunity to build further connections with the content.

Lesson 2: Incorporate Student Assessments in the Planning Process

Student assessment—the third element in the planning triad depicted in Figure 3.1—is an essential aspect of effective planning. Haynie (2006) noted that top teachers use student assessment data in the planning of instruction. Based on data drawn from frequent assessments, effective teachers made data-driven decisions about what goals and objectives to address. Interestingly, both China and U.S. teachers include variations of student assessment in their planning regimens, but the way they go about "beginning with the end in mind" (a concept popularized by Stephen Covey) is strikingly different.

In China, we found teachers' planning attitudes and practices toward student assessment to be focused more on assessing problems that manifest during learning—or, as they often referred to the practice, anticipating (*yùshè* 预设) students' misconceptions. Expert teachers focus more on anticipating the difficulties students might encounter while learning new content rather than on formal assessment—either formative or summative. They also consider students' thinking in order to evaluate the viability of a lesson plan before they modify their instruction.

In the United States, we also found teachers' beliefs and practices to be highly attuned to student assessment but in quite a different manner. They tended to plan with a data orientation in terms of both formative and summative assessment. Whereas teachers in China thought about and planned for so-called learning trouble spots, U.S. teachers were more likely to formally link student learning objectives and assessment in their planning process. Therefore, they are more likely to have assessment in mind while planning instruction.

Lessons from the East

All of the Chinese teachers mentioned that they would visualize themselves in their students' position and predict the learning problems they might have while learning new subject content. They would then plan for that, accordingly. For instance, two teachers stated the following:

> "What is my goal and purpose? What kinds of difficulties and problems are the students likely to encounter? What kinds of questions would the students ask? I make a prediction based on the students' prior knowledge. What kind of teaching methods should I use?"

> "Usually, the night before each lesson, I rehearse my lesson script in my mind like I am playing a movie. I predict what would be the obstacles for students' success in learning or what would make them interested. In this process, I can reveal my potential blind side and address that in my teaching the next day."

Borko and Livingston (1989) investigated the pedagogical expertise in instructional planning by comparing novice and experienced teachers. They found that novice teachers showed more time-consuming, less-efficient planning. While implementing the lessons, their attempts to be responsive to students would likely lead them away from scripted lesson plans. The novice teachers were therefore less successful in translating their instructional plans into action. Expert teachers were better able to predict where in a lesson or course students were likely to have problems and predict misconceptions students were likely to have (as well as areas of learning these misconceptions would affect). This is quite similar to what we found with the Chinese teachers in our study—they paid more attention to predicting student learning problems and accommodating for those problems than did the U.S. teachers in the study.

Lessons from the West

Although none of the Chinese teachers explicitly noted using assessment data as part of their planning process, about half of the U.S. teachers did. High-quality assessments provide teachers with information regarding the extent to which students have attained the intended learning outcomes, and they also inform teachers' instructional decision making (i.e., what to teach and how to teach it). The goals of assessment are both to provide teachers with day-to-day data on students' mental preparedness for certain learning targets and to help teachers make data-based decisions for instruction modification.

Assessment can facilitate instruction and learning in many ways (Gronlund, 2006). In general terms, the value of quality assessment tied to instructional planning can result in the following outcomes:

- Providing diagnostic information regarding students' mental readiness for learning new content.
- Providing formative and summative information needed to monitor student progress and adjust instruction.
- Keeping students motivated.
- Holding students accountable for their own learning.
- Providing opportunities to reexpose students to content.
- Helping students retain and transfer what they have learned.

To exemplify how the inclusion of assessment data can be integral to planning, consider the following comments shared by two U.S. teachers:

"I've recently become more interested in backwards planning. . . . It's a lot easier to just have the essential questions in your mind at this level, and then those are the things that eventually the kids would be able to answer. . . . I have sort of forcibly changed my own lesson planning in the last two years, once I started reading *Understanding by Design* [Wiggins & McTighe, 2005] and thinking a lot more about it. I always have loved planning—it's possibly my favorite part [of teaching]. But I think now the planning's better, and the lessons are better, because I always, always now develop the assessment first."

"So what I do is to deconstruct the test. I go back and I see the latest version of the SAT. . . . I look to see what kinds of things would be measured on that, and I develop . . . specific grammar lessons [based] on those kinds of standardized test questions that I'm positive [students] are likely to encounter."

Lesson Tool:
Practical Tips for Instructional Planning

There are three key questions that teachers need to consider for effective instructional planning (Stronge, 2010):

1. What should be taught?
2. How should it be taught?
3. How should instruction and student learning be assessed?

What should be taught? Effective student learning requires a progressive and coherent set of learning objectives. Effective teachers excel in delineating the intended outcomes of each lesson and describing the behaviors or actions that students should be able to perform after participating in the learning activities. In deciding what should be taught, effective teachers often use prescribed textbooks, but they hardly ever follow traditional plans. In fact, they frequently have blueprints in their minds that have been formed and re-formed over time. Perhaps because of their expertise gained through a continual process of planning, reflecting, and refining, effective teachers are likely to rely on written, formalized lessons—and less than on a well-formed and fluid mental planning model. Expert teachers conceive a lesson along two dimensions:

1. Teacher's own actions, thoughts, and habits.
2. Students' thinking and understanding of the content.

Thus, effective teachers plan not only what to teach but also for whom they are going to teach. They exert effort to reach beyond their comfort zone of disciplinary thinking and actions to incorporate their students' learning needs.

How should it be taught? Once the learning objectives are developed, evidence suggests that expert teachers are more competent than nonexperts at translating their instructional plans into actions. For example, Jones, Jones, and Vermette (2011) noted that a common pitfall for novice teachers in lesson planning is that the learning objective is unclear. Consequently, when lesson objectives are unclear, it becomes quite challenging to move from a nebulous plan to focused instructional delivery. In addition, effective teachers follow a predefined plan while remaining open to changes and continuously adjusting their instruction based on student needs. Furthermore, expert teachers anticipate the difficulties students might encounter while learning the content of a lesson. They consider students' thinking in order to assess the success of a lesson plan and then modify their instruction promptly. Having a lesson plan cannot ensure that the actual lesson will be implemented precisely according to plan; the classroom is full of ebbs and flows. Consequently, teachers need to be opportunistic and tap into their pedagogical and content resources in a fluid and flexible manner in order to proceed smoothly.

How should instruction and student learning be assessed? When learning objectives are established, teachers need to align activities and link the assessment plan to them. Alignment of curriculum, learning activities, and assessment is integral to any instructional design. (This type of alignment is often referred to as the "opportunity to learn.") Before the actual instruction begins, teachers need to decide upon valid and reliable assessment techniques that are available to solicit student learning data and judge the success of the instructional plan. Additionally, teachers should communicate to their students what they are expected to achieve and how they will be assessed after participating in the learning activities.

Lesson 3: Allow Lessons to Follow a Different Path

Both U.S. and Chinese teachers emphasized the fact that they keep their planning open to potential changes and continuously adjust their implementation of the plan based on student needs. Indeed, variation and flexibility in planning and instruction was a key characteristic of how they plan. A majority of all teachers reported that they allow their lessons to deviate from plan and follow a different path (see Figure 3.2).

FIGURE 3.2 Allowing for Variations in Planning

Instructional Planning Strategies	Percentage of Chinese Teachers ($n = 16$)	Percentage of U.S. Teachers ($n = 15$)
Allowing lessons to follow a different path	67%	77%

Lessons from East and West

In an earlier and influential study, both classroom observations and personal interviews indicated that award-winning teachers had fast and accurate pattern recognition capabilities (Berliner, 1986). We found the same quality. The teachers had the skills to recognize patterns in student learning, instantly identify what difficulties their students were having, and make immediate adjustments to their instruction. They were adept at anticipating challenges and difficulties that students were likely to encounter, which enabled them to make contingency plans based on those possibilities. The teachers were also resourceful in the sense that they welcomed changes and used opportunities that occurred along the way to guide their teaching.

Our observations indicated that these teachers used guided questioning techniques to continuously assess students' mastery levels regarding the targeted learning content. Student responses provided important input for teachers to make instructional accommodations, to allow flexibility with their original plans, and to exploit opportunities offered by the immediate circumstances. This was also supported by teachers' comments during interviews.

> "I think that everyone can always grow, but I think sometimes I have to step back and think, 'What can I ask them to make them think through the answer?' . . . Sometimes, with planning, those might be things that I write down, just to keep [the lesson] focused, but I think that over time I've learned to have a variety of questions in the different ranges of thinking that students need. . . . I'm trying to get them to show me what they know, so I try to gear the questions sort of that way. I'm not giving them

the answer when I ask the question but asking them a series of questions to get to aha." *(United States)*

"I use questioning to push my students forward in their learning. My students' responses are often insightful and sometimes shed light on something I never thought about. I could actively take advantage of those opportunities to lead my students to explore more." *(China)*

Detailed planning: Flexible execution. Several of the teachers from both countries commented specifically that with more years of teaching experience, they became more comfortable with allowing lessons to follow a different path than the one they had originally planned. This seemed to be especially true when teachers had confidence in the structure of the lesson and were aware of the possible variations within it. To illustrate, some representative statements included the following:

"I'll put things in front of [my students], and we may take a different path than what I had anticipated. . . . Because I've been teaching the same grade for so long, I understand what I'm supposed to teach, and I'm not afraid to let the kids take me off topic and go down a different path. . . . So my role, I think, is facilitator, guider." *(United States)*

"The standards are written; I follow the standards. I try to organize projects that force the kids to learn those standards or at least part of those standards, but I'm known far and wide—as far and wide as this little school can be—as being the guy who, if something comes up in class that's a learning opportunity (even if it doesn't have anything to do with the Compromise of 1850, for example), then you know what, we're going to take this opportunity, and we're going to learn it." *(United States)*

"I know my students' learning fairly well. My teaching is flexible, and what I am doing is totally contingent upon the students.

For instance, if my students' mastery is not solid enough to move forward to the next step, I would change my original plan. In most cases, I would immediately generate associations with knowledge learned earlier and help students solve their problems. I always enjoy changing tracks and incorporating my students' learning pace and characteristics while implementing a lesson plan." *(China)*

Lesson 4: Use Mental Planning Models

When deciding what should be taught, the exemplary teachers in our study stated that they often unpack prescribed standards and have a blueprint in their minds that they frequently revisit and form and re-form over time. Most of them commented that this mental modeling developed through a combination of experience with and expertise in a specific grade level or content area. Through a constant process of planning, reflecting, and refining, the teachers were able to parlay this experience and knowledge into a deep, rich mental plan for teaching. It's also worth noting that 100 percent of teachers from both countries engaged in some form of mental modeling.

The process of mental planning often replaces more explicit written lesson plans used by less-experienced teachers. Teachers who use mental planning models no longer write meticulous, formalized plans for every lesson. Rather, they rely on a combination of plans from earlier years and a mental planning process that links familiar instruction from the past with the current class and context.

───────── 教师的想法 ─────────

TEACHERS' THOUGHTS ON THE USE
OF MENTAL PLANNING MODELS

United States / 美国

"If I'm starting something new ... I would develop a day-by-day, almost word-by-word lesson plan that would say I'm going to say this, this, this, and this. In the introduction, I'm going to say this, this, this. I'm very detail-oriented when it comes to that. Then, after I've done it two years in a row, I'll have in my mind what questions that I think are appropriate and what extensions I can do to that, so then I'll just be more generic in my daily lesson plan."

"I don't plan! Let me start from square one. I've done this for so many years that I'm kind of an expert at 3rd grade curriculum. But I have fully developed units that have the goals and objectives established, and my lesson plan format is truly Madeline Hunter, to a *T*. I'm always very cognizant of what my anticipatory set will be, how I'm going to have closure, what I'm going to do for a quick evaluation, whether it will be a thumbs up, thumbs down, [or something else]."

(Note: Madeline Hunter's lesson plan template can be characterized as requiring a sequential set of materials/resources: (1) anticipatory set, (2) objective/purpose, (3) instructional input, (4) modeling, (5) checking for understanding, (6) guided practice, and (7) independent practice [Laurier, 2011].)

China / 中国

"[I don't plan] too much in detail. But I have a goal, main points, the difficulties the students may have, and the procedures I will follow."

"I have been teaching for about 13 years. During the first few years, my lesson plans were extremely detailed. I even wrote down what I was going to say during the transition between activities, trying to make sure the flow of the lesson is smooth and the connections between activities are meaningful. If I didn't write it down, I was afraid that I would be lost about what to say—due to nervousness or other reasons. However, for the last few years, I noticed that I changed my approach to lesson planning. I am much more familiar with the flow of my lesson, so I can spend more time thinking about the students rather than just the textbook. Now, my lesson plan is not detailed to the degree that I have to put down every sentence I am going to say. I feel more comfortable about improvising. I think that's a progress for me, because I can communicate with the kids more naturally, instead of putting on a scripted performance like I used to do."

Lessons from East and West

Mental Planning Process. Teachers' comments indicated that the level of detail in lesson planning is contingent upon each teacher's amount of experience and the development of expertise. Relating back to the observational results of these teachers, the activities in their classrooms were well structured, and the routines were obviously institutionalized in their classroom activities. Because the routines had become automated, the teachers could direct their attention and judgment to more important matters, such as differentiating instruction and presenting information in a manner suitable to all students, conducting formative assessments to gauge students' understanding, and responding to necessary changes in real time as the lesson unfolds. John Hattie, in his meta-analysis that included attributes of effective teaching, found that expert teachers use "automaticity so as to free working memory to deal with other more complex characteristics of the situation, whereas experienced non-experts do not optimize the opportunities gained from automaticity" (Hattie, 2003, p. 8).

Expertness in Mental Planning. The teachers in our study, to a person, reflected a high level of expertness that was reflected in their mental planning. Becoming an expert can be characterized by the scaffolding formula reflected in Figure 3.3.

The development of their expertness fits well with Herbert Simon's conception of expertise. According to Simon, a Nobel Prize–winning economist and psychologist, expertise consists of characteristics, skills, and knowledge

FIGURE 3.3   A Process for Building Expertise

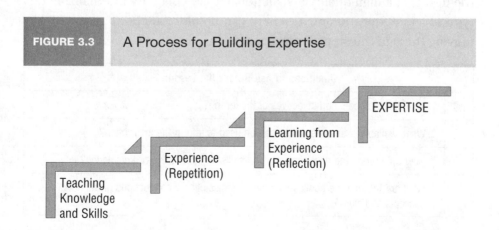

that distinguish experts from novices (Simon & Chase, 1973). A frequently used example for expertise is that of the world-class chess player. A chess expert is thought to have learned about 50,000 "chunks" or chess position patterns. While playing chess, an expert player can efficiently and accurately identify alternative moves and determine the consequences that would result from each alternative. In a similar fashion, after many years of practice and reflection, expert teachers seem capable of storing complex configurations of teaching and learning in their memory. They are thus able to quickly assess various learning situations and make accurate decisions for alternative approaches in dynamic environments.

In order to reach a level of expertness required to plan and execute instructional delivery with the moves of a chess master, continual learners need to reinvent themselves regularly as teachers. Therefore, in a very real sense, they never teach the same lesson twice; their instruction is always fresh and new. In terms of mental planning, they don't have just one move ready for their students; they enter the classroom with a primary goal in mind for their students and, depending on how the lesson unfolds, they can call on a rich, deep array of instructional approaches to achieve the lesson goal.

Lesson Tool:
Checklist for Instructional Planning

The following checklist may be helpful for teachers and instructional supervisors when considering the attributes that should be considered in the design of a high-quality instructional lesson plan. By internalizing this type of lesson questioning, teachers can be more adept at automatically moving through the steps for lesson design.

Questions to Ask Before the Lesson	
☐	1. What are the goals and objectives of the lesson?
☐	2. What available assessment data can be used to inform the instruction?
☐	3. How will I relate the new concepts and skills to students' prior knowledge?
☐	4. What are the real-life applications and interdisciplinary connections of the new concepts and skills?

☐	5. What are the preconceptions or misconceptions that students are likely to make? How will I respond?
☐	6. What strategies will I use to create the "hook" and engage students' attention?
☐	7. Have I gathered, evaluated, or created appropriate instructional materials?
☐	8. What procedures should students follow to ensure content mastery?
☐	9. How much time will I need to teach the different parts of the lesson?
☐	10. What strategies will I use for transitions to maximize instructional time?
☐	11. What major instructional strategies will I use to provide comprehensible instruction?
☐	12. What physical setup of the classroom is most conducive to these instructional strategies?
☐	13. What questions will I ask to monitor student learning during the lesson?
☐	14. What alternative explanations can I provide if students have trouble with concepts or skills?
☐	15. What strategies will I use for reteaching, remediation, or enrichment, if needed?
☐	16. What post-instruction assessment (aligned with the weekly learning objectives) will I use?

教室聚光灯

CLASSROOM SPOTLIGHT

We observed a 9th grade biology teacher in China. All that the teacher brought with her to the classroom was the textbook (developed by the Ministry of Education), which was dog-eared and well used. During the lesson, however, she hardly used it. Rather, she gave clear instructions to her students in terms of which page or paragraph to refer to for information. It seemed as if she had an intimate knowledge of the content in the textbook. During our follow-up interview, the teacher shared that she thinks it is crucial to study the student text and teacher's manual thoroughly in order to deliver classroom instruction successfully.

Lesson 5: Use a Uniform Planning Structure

In short, Chinese teachers followed a highly structured approach to planning, whereas the U.S. teachers did not. To a person, the Chinese teachers in our study adhered to a carefully crafted national approach to designing lessons. Figure 3.4 illustrates distinctions between the teachers in the United States and China in terms of adherence to planning structures.

On its face, it would seem that teachers in the United States were greatly advantaged with the freedom and flexibility they enjoyed—and to a large extent they were—but there are benefits that emerged from the more standardized approach to planning that is followed in China.

Lessons from the East

For this lesson, we only feature the Chinese teachers, since the major findings relate to their planning structure. Though there were common elements that cut across the U.S. teachers' planning structures, their approach to planning was far more variable and individualized.

We found that expert teachers in China and the United States used instructional materials quite differently for planning. Among teachers in China, textbooks and teachers' manuals play an essential role in their work and serve as a primary source of subject-matter and pedagogical knowledge (Fan & Gurcharn, 2000). These materials, carefully developed by the national or provincial Ministry of Education, prescribe not only

| FIGURE 3.4 | Structure in Planning |

Instructional Planning Strategies	Percentage of Chinese Teachers ($n = 16$)	Percentage of U.S. Teachers ($n = 15$)
Follow the textbook and teacher reference book closely	81%	0%
Frame lesson plans around three important concepts: "knowledge points," "key points," and "difficult points"	75%	0%

the learning standards and curriculum but also the exact lessons. (This conformity occurs despite the national government's proclaimed move in 2000 toward a more decentralized approach to educational delivery.) This confirms what Fang and Gopinathan (2009) noticed—countries and cultures that are rooted in a Confucian heritage attach great importance to texts.

Generally, we found this close affiliation with a textbook-driven approach to be somewhat stifling and disadvantageous on various fronts. Among the disadvantages is a reluctance to experiment and a lack of innovation in teaching. Also, it tends to substantially stifle an individual teacher's freedom and creativity. However, one of the advantages of such top-down mandates is that it makes the alignment among curriculum, instruction, and assessment easier and more efficient. We found that the Chinese teachers were thriving even with the imposed constraints. They were adept not only at meeting the content coverage requirements within the framework of the prescribed pacing but also in using curriculum guidance to scaffold instruction according to student ability and progress. The assigned textbooks and reference books seemed to free up more time for these teachers to pay more attention to their students and consider how to deliver each lesson more effectively.

Another clear aspect of the Chinese structure is that teachers frame their lesson plans around three important points. These three elements are fundamental to their approach (Tsui & Wong, 2009):

• **Knowledge points** (*zhīshi diǎn* 知识点) refer to all of the facts, ideas, concepts, skills, or procedures that are covered by a specific lesson. Some of these points may have already been taught and will only be briefly reviewed in the current lesson; some may be too challenging for students to tackle completely.

• **Key points** (*zhòng diǎn* 重点) are the primary learning objectives that will be explicitly taught and mastered.

• If key points are identified through unpacking the curriculum, then **difficult points** (*nán diǎn* 难点) have to be identified from an understanding of students' prior knowledge of the subject matter and learning habits.

Based on a review of lesson plan artifacts, we noticed that all Chinese teachers included descriptions of key points and difficult points in their lesson plans. This means that the teachers need to

1. Develop a systematic understanding about the scope and depth of the learning standards in the curriculum.
2. Spell out aspects of the topic or concepts that will be learned in each lesson.
3. Predict where students are likely to stumble, based on knowledge of their prior learning.

教室聚光灯

CLASSROOM SPOTLIGHT

In addition to identifying the knowledge points, key points, and difficult points in their lesson plans, many Chinese teachers communicated these points to their students in order to promote student metacognition. For instance, while introducing a new lesson, a 3rd grade teacher stated, "The key point of your learning in this lesson is dividing fractions. I know you've mastered whole-number division, the concept of fractions, and the multiplication of fractions. Today you will learn the invert-and-multiply algorithm, which will help you solve problems that involve divisions of fractions really fast. *But* it is really easy to develop misconceptions of the procedures, so the difficult point today is probably about developing a conceptual understanding of the process with its underlying meanings."

This excerpt of one teacher's talk indicates that the mathematics teacher we observed in China uses sophisticated language to build a solid conceptual understanding of fraction divisions. We noticed that Chinese teachers tend to use abstract frameworks to conceptualize math problems and tasks, and students seem to enjoy these high-level conceptual explanations. Similar findings are evident in previous studies of mathematics instruction in China (e.g., An, Kulm, & Wu, 2004; Stevenson & Stigler, 1992).

Lesson 6: Plan Collaboratively or Embrace Individual Autonomy

The primary takeaway from this lesson—at least for us—is that Chinese teachers plan collaboratively whereas U.S. teachers plan with a high degree of individual autonomy. A large percentage of the U.S. teachers, while following curricular requirements in a more general sense, exercised considerable latitude to customize, individualize, and operate as independent agents in the planning and implementation of instruction (Figure 3.5).

Beyond the striking differences in how U.S. and Chinese teachers handle collaboration versus individuality, what makes these findings so interesting is that both approaches have substantial and sustained benefits. We will explore each, in turn, here.

Lessons from the East

All of the Chinese teachers worked in collaborative groups, and the pressure to keep up with the pace of their peers' classrooms seemed to deprive them of the ability to be flexible and autonomous. Such strict pacing—which was a by-product of the deliberative collaborative planning—mandated a fixed amount of time each day in which formal instruction of certain lesson or concepts would occur. However, a considerable amount of their planning time was spent studying the text and teacher's manual—either individually or collaboratively with colleagues—and this collaborative approach to planning revealed its own benefits.

All of the teachers were involved in some kind of collaborative team, which engaged them in a recursive cycle of studying the curriculum, textbook, and teacher's reference book; planning the lesson; implementing

FIGURE 3.5	Structure in Planning

Instructional Planning Strategies	Percentage of Chinese Teachers ($n = 16$)	Percentage of U.S. Teachers ($n = 15$)
Autonomy and creativity in planning	0%	61%

the lesson; and discussing and revising their plan for instruction. They all agreed that team planning is an effective way to

- Share resources.
- Increase their understanding of the framework of the curriculum and textbook.
- Reduce their workload.
- Build stronger collegial networks.
- Improve the quality of a lesson plan.

Teachers usually grouped together according to subject and grade level to study the curriculum, textbooks, and teacher's reference books. Such collaboration allowed them to see the curriculum in its entirety and avoid overemphasizing one area of content at the expense of others (Chan & Rao, 2010). Stigler and Stevenson (1991) observed that teachers in China, fostered by a culture that values collegiality over individualism, have a tradition of planning together and observing one another's lessons. Such a culture of collaboration has enabled teachers to pull together their teaching ideas and resources. It's also true that teachers in China have, if not a lighter workload, certainly a different workload than their U.S. counterparts. Chinese teachers teach larger class sizes, with the average class in China being around 50 students. However, they teach far fewer lessons per week. This concentration of students in larger classes, in combination with different scheduling methods, gives Chinese teachers far more time to observe one another's classes, conduct action research, and engage in collaborative planning.

Furthermore, since all of our interviews were conducted in teachers' offices, we had the opportunity to observe that, in each of the schools we visited, teachers in the same subject (and, in some cases, the same grade level) were situated in the same office to facilitate collaboration. In many instances, their office desks were even grouped together to foster a group mentality and collegial workplace. This physical proximity facilitates collective learning and promotes teachers' engagement in conversations of their daily practices (Fang, Hooghart, Song, & Choi, 2003). In addition, this workplace culture allows teachers to refine their craft together and engage in continuous professional improvement (Fang & Gopinathan, 2009; Paine, 1990). By comparison, Haynie (2006) also examined the practices of a range of U.S. biology teachers, whose effectiveness was identified by their students' achievement gains. Most top teachers collaborated with one or more teachers while planning lessons; however, the bottom teachers reported that they always planned lessons alone.

Benefits to Collaborative Lesson Planning

The benefits of collaboration and team planning are clear and compelling. In fact, the extant research is replete with examples of how team planning impacts teacher effectiveness, including the following findings:

- Teachers who are engaged in collaborative planning, teaching, observing, revising, and reteaching lessons can
    - Increase their knowledge of subject matter.
    - Increase their knowledge of instruction.
    - Increase their ability to observe students.
    - Build stronger collegial networks.
    - Enhance their ability to connect daily practice to long-term goals.
    - Maintain a strong sense of motivation and sense of efficacy.
    - Improve the quality of their lesson plans (Lewis, Perry, & Hurd, 2004).
- Planning time is important for teachers to develop thought-provoking lessons. Teachers who plan longer—both individually or collaboratively—use a wider variety of instructional strategies and use them more frequently (Lookabill, 2008).
- There is a significant positive correlation between collaboration and lesson plans that result in higher scores from the Student Teacher Assessment Instrument (Taylor, 2004).

Lessons from the West

Our study of U.S. teachers revealed that they have far more autonomy in deciding what and how they will teach. One teacher commented on the amount of creativity allowed in her lesson planning:

> "Now it's like I need those outcomes, indicators, essential questions. That's what I need to start with in order to be creative, you know, so I need to know what they need to know and be able to do. I have my little guides that basically just give me

the objectives—they give me lessons, too, but I don't like to use the lessons in the guide. Some of them are good, and I start there, but I find out what my kids enjoy, what speaks to them, what speaks to me, and I create my lessons."

As noted earlier, all of the Chinese teachers mentioned that they would follow the textbook and teacher's reference book closely, both of which were developed by the Ministry of Education. By contrast, teachers in the United States enjoyed more flexibility and autonomy with respect to pacing, selection of learning materials, and content goals—as long as they are in alignment with the overall curriculum and standards.

These teachers valued the autonomy they were afforded to make decisions about instructional materials. State-mandated curricula in the United States usually do not specify which lessons must take place in the classroom. Therefore, individual teachers have freedom to sequence units and lessons in their own ways and to develop appropriate timelines for the completion of those plans. Interestingly, research supports the idea that autonomy is a critical component for teacher growth and career satisfaction (Conley, Muncy, & You, 2005; Johnson, 1990; Mangin, 2005).

Alexander (2002) argued that U.S. teachers value independence, individualism, and decision-making autonomy over schedule, curriculum, and classroom management. Some researchers also stress that this autonomy should be neither perceived nor employed as permission to avoid cooperating with one's colleagues, which could lead to professional isolation (Pearson & Moomaw, 2005).

A different study of top U.S. teachers found that the teachers were not restricted by pacing guides and reached beyond prepared resources to plan their own activities, whereas most of their less-effective (and less-successful) colleagues used resources already prepared (Haynie, 2006). In still another study, Allington and Johnston (2000) found that the instruction of effective teachers was multisourced. What does this mean? Exemplary teachers are inclined to stretch the reading and writing beyond the textbooks. Although they still use prescribed textbooks, effective teachers rarely follow traditional plans for these materials. For instance, while planning for a lesson in social science, an effective teacher might use historical fiction, biography, information from the Internet and in magazines, and other nontraditional sources.

By contrast, Liu and Meng (2008) found that responsibility and dedication are regarded as the two most important qualities of successful Chinese teachers. Among the bottom-ranked qualities across all groups? Creativity. In another study of Chinese teachers, Liu (2006) uncovered similar findings, including the following factors:

- Chinese teaching behaviors are more uniform across classes.
- Effective instruction in China emphasizes whole-class activities over small-group activities.
- Demonstration/lecture is the most popular instructional strategy.
- All Chinese teachers try to maximize instruction time due to the exam-driven system in which students' test scores are critical to teachers' evaluations.

Although we are discussing lessons from U.S. teachers in this section, we felt it might be useful to see the Chinese teachers' comparative emphasis on uniformity noted in the above list. A fair comparison of Chinese uniformity versus U.S. individuality with regard to planning practices is depicted in Figures 3.6 and 3.7.

Caveat: Time to Plan (or Not)

It's never simple to make straightforward comparisons with a topic as complex as what makes a teacher effective. Add to that complexity the uniqueness of the cultural contexts in which teachers in the United States and China teach, and we begin to understand the challenges of conducting a meaningful and fair comparative analysis.

Though we built the foundation for *West Meets East* on an international comparative analysis and related extant research, it is important to keep in mind that we are not always comparing apples to apples. This issue holds true for our discussion in this chapter about teacher planning. Thus, it is vitally important to understand that significant structural differences exist between the educational systems in both countries.

One specific example of a contextual and cultural difference between the United States and China is class size; another is the amount of time allocated for planning. One of the trade-offs of large class sizes in China

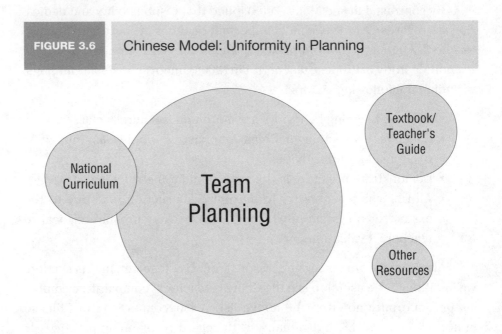

FIGURE 3.6 Chinese Model: Uniformity in Planning

National Curriculum

Team Planning

Textbook/ Teacher's Guide

Other Resources

FIGURE 3.7 U.S. Model: Individuality in Planning

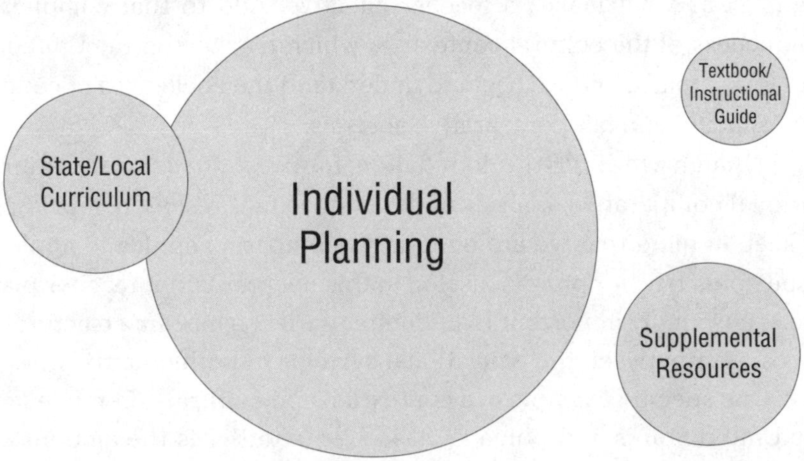

State/Local Curriculum

Individual Planning

Textbook/ Instructional Guide

Supplemental Resources

is a lighter workload in terms of the number of courses taught per week, thereby generating more time for planning. In a typical Chinese school schedule, lessons are short (45–50 minutes each), and each teacher typically teaches only one subject area—but multiple times to multiple classes. A typical teacher in China teaches 12–16 lessons per week.

By contrast, a typical teacher in the United States spends a vast majority of his or her time engaged in instructional delivery. U.S. teachers are typically allocated one hour to plan and about five hours to teach each day (Kennedy, 2010). The ratio of planning time to instructional time is around 1:5. In other words, there are around 10–12 minutes available to plan for an hour's instruction.

In the United States, teacher planning time is sparse, particularly at the elementary level where teachers usually teach multiple subjects— reading, mathematics, science, and social studies. Moreover, the "one hour" available for planning is also the only official time teachers have to correct student work, diagnose learning difficulties, communicate with parents or school specialists, and complete paperwork that may or may not be related to classroom instruction.

In China, the ratio of planning time to instructional time is closer to 1:2 (Kennedy, 2010). In addition, the centralized curriculum and the philosophy of collectivism in Chinese culture provide favorable conditions for collaboration in instructional planning. Figure 3.8 could help illuminate the unique differences between U.S. and Chinese teachers in terms of teaching loads and instructional planning time.

Summary

While planning instruction, teachers in both countries tend to emphasize the alignment between curriculum standards and instruction, but U.S. teachers go further and incorporate assessment in their planning processes. Chinese teachers stress that they develop and test hypotheses about students' learning difficulties, and they anticipate students' misconceptions while planning. In addition, they identify key points and difficult points in their planning process for each lesson. By contrast, U.S. teachers have more autonomy in their planning, and they value such self-governance. They have

FIGURE 3.8	Time for Teaching and Planning

Features	Chinese Teachers	U.S. Teachers
Average Class Size	50	20
Average Number of Classes Taught per Week	12–15	25
Average Number of Students Taught per Week	600–750	500
Teaching Time per Week	12 hours	25 hours
Planning Time per Week	24 hours	5 hours
Unique Features That Affect Instructional Planning	• Larger classes • Fewer classes • More planning time	• Smaller classes • More classes • Less planning time

the most flexibility in designing lesson units and assigning timelines based on the needs, strengths, and interests of their students.

So what's the bottom line? Award-winning teachers in China and the United States are far more alike than they are different. There are clear strengths shared by the teachers in the two countries. Additionally, there are lessons to be learned by understanding how and why they are different in their respective approaches to planning. If we can emulate and integrate the planning strengths of these extraordinary teachers, then we, undoubtedly, will have better instructional planning, better instructional delivery, a better understanding of the needs of our students, and, consequently, better student learning.

4

Instructional Practice

第四章：课堂教学

Before, I sought to make teaching methods distinctive from each other. I have a clear list of instructional methods, and number one is this, number two is that, and number three is that. Gradually, I started to realize that the best teaching is markless/traceless [wúhén 无痕]. I am still striving to achieve this, but I'm not very good at it yet. I think the best teaching occurs when the students are learning but without noticing that they are taught to. Ideally, instructional methods should be embedded in the teaching and learning process. —Chinese teacher

If I had in my mind that I needed to be [my students'] instructor and they needed to adapt to what it is that I want them to learn, then they're not going to learn as much as they can. —U.S. teacher

Say the word *teacher,* and the many pictures that spring to mind probably include at least some images of a person writing on a chalkboard, talking or reading to a large group of children seated at desks, pointing to someone with a hand raised to speak, or otherwise doing the most visible work of teaching. Teaching, of course, involves much more than instructional delivery. For instance, as we discussed in Chapter 2, relationships may actually matter much more than lesson plans in what we remember about our teachers beyond our school years. Nevertheless, instructional delivery is at the center of the work of teaching, and it forms the majority of teachers' interactions with students and people's preconceived notions of what teaching is all about.

Instructional delivery is also the point at which all other aspects of teaching tend to converge and allow teachers to demonstrate high levels of expertise. The teacher's preparation and planning, the relationships maintained with students, and the structures established to manage the classroom environment—all of these threads are brought together, successfully or not, during instructional delivery.

Many of the descriptions we present in this book about teachers and their work in both the United States and in China come from the teachers' own voices and the reflections they provided in our interviews with them, yet we also observed all of the teachers as they implemented one or more lessons in their classrooms. This chapter, then, reflects on what we observed in teachers' classrooms and on what they said about their own instructional delivery. The following are the key themes related to instructional delivery that emerged from this work. We found that award-winning teachers

1. Use a wide *variety of instructional activities* and *assessment strategies* that address a range of cognitive levels.
2. Sustain *high levels of student engagement* while keeping themselves as the learning director.
3. Maintain *high levels of flexibility and responsiveness* to classroom circumstances and student response.
4. Attend to the needs of students of varying ability levels through *differentiation.*
5. Create and maintain a *safe, fun, and intellectually stimulating learning environment.*

These emphases were evident among all teachers in both countries, yet we noted some significant differences in the patterns. In the remainder of this chapter, we discuss each theme with reference to some of those key similarities and differences across classrooms and countries.

教室聚光灯

CLASSROOM SPOTLIGHT

One of the teachers we observed is also the principal of a middle school with 2,100 students in Lijiang, China. Lijiang is a historical city that is about 800 years old and located in the Himalayan foothills of Yunnan Province. The school we visited is home to approximately 60 percent Han Chinese and 35–36 percent Naxi (a minority group concentrated in Lijiang), with other minority groups making up the rest of the students. The principal is also a math teacher and has been honored by the Ministry of Education with an award for teaching excellence. When we visited the school, he was teaching 8th grade algebra to a classroom of 65 students. During our visit, we observed how his instructional strategies address the unique learning and support needs of minority and at-risk students. Thus, even with a large classroom packed wall to wall with middle school students, he was planning for differentiated instruction—particularly by grouping and asking different levels of questions.

Lesson 1: Incorporate a Variety of Instructional Activities That Target a Range of Cognitive Levels

Teachers use a wide range of instructional strategies to support student learning, guide students to a deeper understanding of content, and address the needs of specific learners. In our observations, we paid particular attention to the types of instructional activities teachers employed, using an observation instrument that involved noting all activities used within discrete five-minute segments (Cassady et al., 2004). During these observations, we also noted the levels of cognitive demand involved in each of the segments, using the revised version of Bloom's taxonomy—remembering, understanding, applying, analyzing, evaluating, and creating (Anderson & Krathwohl, 2001). Possible ratings for the cognitive levels within each five-minute segment were *not evident, evident,* and *well represented.*

During our follow-up interviews, we asked teachers to talk about their instructional strategies. We wanted them to describe their preferred approaches, explain how their instructional choices reflect their specific content areas, discuss their responses to the range of students in their classrooms, and evaluate their own questioning practices. Naturally, even in questions that did not specifically target these aspects of instruction, the teachers referred to their instructional practices as the centerpiece of their overall professional work.

The most notable finding about instructional activities across teachers' classrooms was the variety that was employed. On average, teachers used nine identified activities within lessons that lasted an average of about 52–59 minutes. Nine! At first blush, this might appear to be a lot; however, what we actually found is that these activities flowed together seamlessly during the course of a lesson. In addition, there were clear connections in how and when instructional activities were used. Some activities were used simultaneously within specific segments; for example, *questioning* and *student responding* generally occurred together. Figure 4.1 provides a list of the most prominent instructional activities used by teachers in each country.

In addition to this overall variety, several patterns emerged from our observations of and interviews with teachers in the two countries:

• There is a very high use of questioning and student response in both countries. All of the teachers used questioning and student response to questions as frequent strategies, and several teachers commented that

FIGURE 4.1	Top Five Instructional Activities Used by Award-Winning Teachers

China	United States
Questioning	Questioning
Student Responding	Student Responding
Lecture	Work with Individual Students
Technology Use by Teacher	Work with Groups of Students
Lecture with Discussion	Lecture

questioning was one of the most important tools in their classrooms. Teachers also reflected on the quality of their questioning practices, and these responses revealed their focus on using questioning in specific ways to build and support student learning and to assess student understanding.

- There is variation in teachers' use of lectures and small-group work. Teachers in China relied on lecturing much more than their counterparts in the United States did, and U.S. teachers were more likely to make use of small-group work and interact with small groups and individuals on a one-on-one basis. Teachers in both countries spoke of the ways that their own understanding of the content and their desire to support student engagement informed their choices of strategies and grouping approaches.

- Teachers demand a range of cognitive levels from their students. Teachers implemented various instructional activities that addressed a range of demand, even though their approaches were usually classified as addressing remembering and understanding levels (as opposed to higher levels of cognitive demand). To some degree, this reflected a perspective that teachers would encourage students to activate their knowledge and comprehension as a starting point for any activity.

———————————— 教师的想法 ————————————

TEACHERS' REFLECTIONS ON QUESTIONING

China / 中国

"I think questioning is an important teaching method. [In a recent discussion] about it, we found that an effective teacher and a mediocre teacher have significant differences in their design of questions."

———————•———————

"I think the problem in my questioning is my underestimation of my students. Many times I have preconception [*yùxiǎng* 预想] that my students are only able to answer the question to this certain level, but it turns out that they can give quite comprehensive and deep answers."

United States / 美国

"I don't think I do a very good job at questioning. I am working on that. I am an old teacher, and it is so tempting to ask questions that have a definite answer, and I am working very hard to avoid that."

———•———

"I'm a good questioner [but] a bad waiter for the answer-er."

———•———

"We do a lot of questioning and a lot of asking. . . . I try to think about what I need to know from them. I don't always do a great job, but I try not to tell kids what they need to know. I try to ask them and see if they figured it out yet."

Lessons from the East

Lessons in Chinese classrooms tended to be more structured overall and more similar in structure from one classroom to another than those in the United States. Chinese teachers demonstrated a much more extensive use of lecturing than their U.S. counterparts, and they integrated a frequent use of questioning within that context. They also described very structured approaches to questioning, emphasizing the way they used questions to build students from lower-order to higher-order thinking:

> "When I design questions, I always start with the easiest ones. They can be so easy that every student can answer. Then the questions move from easier ones to more challenging ones."

———•———

> "No matter what lesson mode you adopt, it should have a progressive process from shallow to deep, from lower level to higher level. For this process, I would build a chain of questions that can guide [*yǐndǎo* 引导] student learning."

The instructional activities of questioning, student responding, and lecturing were observed in all of the Chinese teachers' classrooms and in over 80 percent of the observed lesson segments. Likewise, in both observations and interviews, teachers emphasized textbooks as central to their teaching and explained how key learning experiences were organized around the textbook. More than 80 percent of teachers had their students working independently during our observations, although this occurred in only about 32 percent of the total observed segments. This means that independent student work was used by most teachers, but it was used sparingly.

Several teachers explained that they sensed their profession was moving away from traditional lecture-style teaching, and many also commented on their perceptions of the value of hands-on, inquiry learning. They emphasized stimulating students' interests and making connections to students' lives but also while staying within the specific guidelines of the texts.

"We feel that our classroom is still dominated by traditional examination-oriented strategies. The nation is seriously promoting creativity and innovation, [and it is] advocating for the cultivation of students' ability to create and innovate. I think we are making progress."

"In my opinion, the teacher should ask questions that are value-added—the questions that deserve to be thought over and answered. The questions should be able to stimulate students' interest or should be related to their real life."

"For teaching strategies, I prefer to use multiple types of activities, rather than just seatwork and reading the text. For instance, a field trip to the supermarket is an authentic learning activity to learn the content. I think when the students are engaged in various activities to learn the subject, the outcomes are generally better than just monotonously reading/reciting the texts."

Lessons from the West

All of the teachers we visited in the United States, like the teachers in China, used questioning and student response during their lessons, although they used these strategies in a somewhat lower percentage of lesson segments (just over 60 percent). Only 57 percent of teachers used lecturing, and this strategy was only observed in 17 percent of lesson segments. The teachers demonstrated a stronger emphasis on small-group work and on interacting with students in a small-group or individualized context.

In their interviews, teachers emphasized engaging students in authentic learning experiences and real-world problem solving. Although they were noted by teachers in both countries as valuable activities, these areas of focus appeared to a somewhat greater degree with U.S. teachers. This emphasis on authenticity is reflected to some extent in slightly higher average ratings for evidence of application, evaluation, and creation among levels of cognitive demand in U.S. classrooms, although the numbers were fairly similar overall (Figure 4.2).

According to their own descriptions, teachers in the United States are less formalized and structured in their questioning techniques. Several teachers alluded to structuring a sequence of questions, but such a systematic approach was emphasized considerably less than with teachers in China. Nevertheless, they either felt confident in their questioning or at

FIGURE 4.2 Cognitive Levels of Instructional Activities by Country

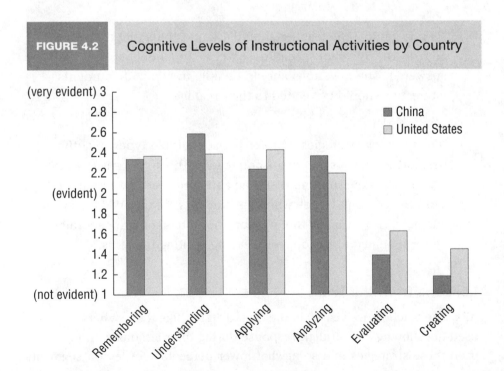

least confident in the ways in which they were continually working to grow and strengthen their questioning practices.

> "I like how I ask questions. And if there was one thing that I tell my student teachers to pay attention to—I've had 26 student teachers now—is to listen to how I ask questions."

———————————•———————————

> "I'm sometimes not as intentional about going up in an order where I've got a high-level question at the top and asking some inference-level questions that would scaffold [toward] that . . . so I kind of have a question pyramid in my mind which I think about, but I think there are some gaps there that I could improve. I think I'm at the point where I know where I need to improve, which is probably better than I was 10 years ago."

———————————— 教室聚光灯 ————————————

CLASSROOM SPOTLIGHT

A high school English teacher in the United States worked at a school with a high population of children of migrant families. The students had selected books to read based on their interests and were placed in groups. Some students were reading *Life of Pi* while others were reading *Friday Night Lights*. Rather than lecture about symbolism or character traits, the teacher developed guiding questions for small-group discussion around symbolism and character traits. The teacher circulated around the room, stopping at each group to interject a comment or ask a question. Finally, the groups convened as a whole class, and one spokesperson from each group shared that group's findings.

Lesson Tool:
Self-Questioning Your Questioning Practice

Research on teachers' questioning practices and their perceptions of those practices has demonstrated that, very often, perceptions do not match reality (Walsh & Sattes, 2005). In general, teachers tend to ask a greater number of lower-level questions and many more managerial questions than they might perceive. Teachers also tend to ask far more questions than their students do, answering many of their own questions and talking for a far greater percentage of time (Coleman, 2006; Tienken, Goldberg, & DiRocco, 2009). One of the most illuminating and instructive exercises a teacher can do to prompt reflection is to examine samples of his or her own questioning in action.

Researchers, teachers, and others involved with professional development in education have constructed many different ways of classifying questions. Among the more popular approaches would be to contrast open- and closed-ended questions and higher- and lower-level questions (Nystrand & Gamoran, 1991; Piccolo, Harbaugh, Carter, Capraro, & Capraro, 2008; Reinsvold & Cochran, 2012; Soter et al., 2008). We can also classify questions as those that require interpretation or synthesis versus those that require simple recall. Any of these systems of classification may provide a useful organizer for examining and reflecting on questioning in practice.

Consider recording (audio or video) one or more lessons and writing down the questions you ask. Use the tally sheet in Figure 4.3 to document

FIGURE 4.3	Questioning Analysis Tool

Question	Type		Level of Thinking		Complexity of Response	
	closed-ended	open-ended	lower	higher	*yes*/*no*	thoughtful response

the types of questions you ask according to one or more of the following considerations:

- How many questions are open-ended, and how many are closed-ended?
- How many questions are posed in ways that prompt higher-level thinking versus lower-level thinking?
- How many questions are answerable by *yes* or *no?* For how many of those were further follow-up questions asked?
- How many questions were followed by further questions or encouragement for additional thinking or explanation from students?

CLASSROOM SPOTLIGHT

A 4th grade enrichment teacher in the United States was observed guiding her students through an activity that was focused on statistics using data from fantasy football. Her discussion of the lesson emphasized two main components: using interest to promote student engagement and trusting students to develop their responses to the task somewhat on their own (without step-by-step directions). She used student interest in football as a starting place for real-world connections and for getting students invested in ongoing data collection and analysis. She also explained the parameters she had laid out at the beginning of the project as well as the areas she had left open for independent decision making (with some guidance). Furthermore, she explained how she found ways to make connections with the content to build her own enthusiasm as an important basis for communicating that level of engagement with her students.

Lesson 2: Deliver Student-Centered, Teacher-Directed Instruction That Promotes Student Engagement

Teaching, at its heart, is a highly interactive activity, involving the interplay of how teachers and students engage with the material and each other. While conducting our observations in China and the United States, we noted not only the teachers' behaviors as described earlier but also the level of student engagement that was evident throughout. Specifically—and again relying on our observation instrument—we noted the percentage of students who appeared to be engaged during each five-minute segment of observation.

Evidence of engagement included such behaviors as responding to questions, looking at the teacher or the materials as directed, writing, and other such actions that reflected the types of engagement the lesson segment warranted. Within each segment, we also noted who was primarily directing the learning activity: the teacher or the students. The teachers spoke frequently in their interviews on different aspects of student engagement and involvement in the learning process. Throughout our observations and interviews, we found several key patterns:

- There were high levels of student engagement. Students appeared, in general, to be highly engaged in lessons, across all of the instructional strategies noted earlier. Teachers also described ways of promoting engagement within their lessons by incorporating such elements as novelty, interest, connections, and humor.
- There were high levels of teacher direction. In the majority of the classrooms we observed, the teacher was the learning director of the lesson. Teachers promoted high student engagement, as noted above, and spoke frequently of the importance of teaching in a student-centered manner, yet they remained the learning directors.
- There was an emphasis on connections with students' lives and interests. One aspect of this emphasis that emerged from our observations and interviews was the value that teachers placed on connecting with students' own lives and interests as a way of promoting connections to the content and fostering deeper, more authentic learning.

教师的想法

TEACHERS' THOUGHTS ON STUDENT-CENTERED CLASSROOMS AND STUDENT ENGAGEMENT

China / 中国

"In my opinion, students should be the owner of the classroom, so I strive to facilitate my students and motivate them to participate in [*cānyù* 参与

or *róngrù* 融入] the learning activities more actively. In every lesson, I do my best to make every student engaged with learning and immersed in [*tóurù* 投入] a positive learning environment."

"If it is just lecturing, the students will forget what they memorized soon. However, if you involve them in authentic/hands-on learning activities that make sense, they will remember it for their whole lives."

United States / 美国

"I want them to be in charge. I want the kids to be in charge of their learning and not me."

"You also noticed that I was not interested in explaining my opinions but in their opinions and why they thought the way they did. So it has to do with trying to get yourself off center stage and get the kids to do most of the talking. That's really critical."

"I've played in my classroom for years, and I've always told my students that we're going to have a good time because I don't do boring; I don't know how to do boring, and I want them to enjoy themselves."

Lessons from the East

Instruction in the Chinese teachers' classrooms tended to be more teacher-centered than in the United States, and the emphasis was on lecture and teacher demonstration. Keep in mind, though, that the teacher was clearly the learning director in most aspects of lessons in both countries. Our results supported previous studies that found the salient feature of classrooms in countries with a strong Confucian heritage was the teacher's dominance of the teaching and learning process (Hiebert et al., 2003; Huang & Leung, 2004); yet our study and these previous studies also demonstrated high levels of student engagement within teacher-centered classrooms. Other work has also indicated that teacher-centered classrooms and large classes may not necessarily translate into passive learning or learning at low cognitive levels (Chan & Rao, 2010).

> "I don't know how the teachers in other nations teach, but based on my understanding of classroom instruction in China, lecturing doesn't necessarily mean that the teacher does all the talking in the classroom and the students have to be passive listeners. That's not true. Teachers have been experimenting painstakingly to stimulate students to learn actively, explore, and participate in group discussions."

Many teachers commented in their interviews that they saw the teacher's role in the classroom as a facilitator or guide, and they encouraged students to take the initiative for their own learning. They spoke of using humor and connections with students' lives as ways of facilitating engagement and initiative and explained their own professional growth over time to increase such engagement.

> "Our current ideology of instruction is oriented toward student-centered learning and enhancing students' enthusiasm for learning. The teacher is the organizer and guide. The teacher is here to prompt and improve student learning and to provide support when the students need it."

> "The best way to teach is to let students learn the knowledge by themselves. If the students are not interested, no matter how good the teachers are at explaining and lecturing, it will be futile. Therefore, I think if I can stimulate and inspire [*jīfā* 激发] my students to take initiative to learn, their learning will surely be successful."

> "I used to be just like I am here—I am teaching, I am presenting the content from the textbook, and I am doing what the textbook prescribed. But now I engage the students in authentic learning activities and hands-on activities to let them learn from experience."

The teachers also emphasized that their decisions regarding how to center and direct their instruction and promote student engagement often depended on the specific content and their assessment of students' learning progress.

"But of course, the decision of instructional strategies is contingent upon the specific learning content. In the lesson you just observed, I only spent a very small amount of time in group learning, because I felt group learning among the students themselves cannot make them reach the desired learning outcomes. There was a need for the teacher to come in to lecture and give some directions. If I solely depended on the strategy of group learning, I am afraid the level of student learning would be shallow."

———————•———————

"I realize that teachers should be the guide or facilitator. The teacher's job is to initiate the problem, then to stimulate students to think and solve the problem by themselves. I found this type of instruction was much more effective. Physics is a discipline based on experiments. Sometimes, no matter how hard you try, verbal explanations cannot make experiments clear. The best way to deliver instruction is to ask students to explore and experience themselves."

—————————— 教室聚光灯 ——————————
CLASSROOM SPOTLIGHT

We observed a 9th grade math lesson in Beijing, China. During the 45-minute observation period, we found that the teacher relied heavily on instructional strategies for the whole class without much individualization. However, she was highly consistent in communicating with clarity and providing plentiful instructional examples and guided practice. The instruction was characterized by high content density and a fast pace. In addition, most of the student learning involved complex mathematical thinking, with the students continuously engaged in identifying problems, posing reasonable solutions, giving details of their thinking processes, and providing justification for their answers. The teacher used questions and student responses to elicit and interpret students' ideas and to understand what students found confusing or difficult. She promptly provided alternative explanations, models, and procedures to represent core concepts or skills. In this dynamic interaction, the teacher created a responsive and flexible classroom environment by bringing together the knowledge of the explanatory frameworks that organize and connect content and her students' knowledge in order to make necessary adjustments "on the fly." This skill of listening to what students say and constructing appropriate adaptive responses on a moment-to-moment basis was truly an exemplary demonstration of teaching expertise.

Lessons from the West

Although teachers in both countries mentioned the importance of student-centered instruction, classrooms in the United States were a little more observably student-centered than those in China. Teachers in the United States tended to emphasize more student exploration during lessons and to engage students in active problem-solving tasks, building toward an understanding of concepts and a development of skills—rather than conveying information and moving toward exploration once content was more thoroughly understood. The different approach in the two countries in part reflects differences in beliefs and attitudes about learning and the most effective approach to achieving learning goals. As noted previously, though, classrooms in both countries demonstrated high student engagement and various levels of cognitive demand. The following comment illustrates the pattern we observed in U.S. classrooms around supporting student exploration as a step toward learning and understanding new content:

> "I really stress student ownership of what they're learning. I present the material and try and let them share the big idea rather than me telling them what the big idea is. I try to set up situations where they stumble upon it, like 'Ta-da, here it is.' They tend to remember it better if they have experienced it and discovered it on their own."

In addition, teachers in the United States placed a somewhat greater emphasis on student self-expression, and they frequently commented on the importance of making learning meaningful and of drawing connections between classroom content and students' own lives.

> "Some things are fun, but not everything. Some things are just hard work. And so I'll tell [my students] straight up that this is hard work, but why do you need to know this? Here's why you need to know it. And then [I'll] show them how good writers use all of this stuff and then give them examples of why it's important. You change the whole message."

Lesson Tool:
Recognizing Engagement

The observation instrument in our study prompted us to note, at regular intervals, the percentage of students who were engaged with the lesson. As a research team, we defined several specific types of behaviors that we would designate as representing engagement. Consider for yourself: What are some of the signs that teachers can use to assess engagement?

Study the collection of adjectives in Figure 4.4. What evidence would suggest that each could be applied to an individual student or group of students? What reaction (positive or negative) might such evidence prompt from a teacher? If a colleague observed your class, which of these adjectives would he or she use to describe your students? What is an example of an action or inaction that exemplifies each adjective?

FIGURE 4.4	Adjectives for Describing Students		
engaged	entertained	off-task	disengaged
on-task	attentive	bored	inattentive
focused	compliant	defiant	restless
invested	involved	anxious	removed

Many of these words are quite common in the educational community, yet perhaps we do not always define them fully to ourselves as we think about our goals for student involvement. As you review your lessons, consider which terms apply to which students, and reflect upon and discuss with colleagues ways to promote those behaviors that are most conducive to learning.

Lesson 3: Embrace Flexibility and Responsiveness

Teaching practices among our study participants were characterized by a strong emphasis on flexibility and responsiveness in instruction. The teachers commented on the importance of being alert during instruction and the need to make decisions within a lesson about particular directions to take based on student response. Such flexibility and responsiveness require both good planning overall, as noted in Chapter 3, and a willingness to depart from a lesson plan to serve the larger learning outcomes. Several key points are important to note here from our observations and interviews:

• Deep content knowledge is important to promote nimble shifts in instruction. When teachers spoke of their decisions to take lessons in a different direction based on aspects of student response, those decisions were grounded in a clear vision of the intended learning outcomes and what kinds of shifts were most appropriate while ensuring a thorough understanding of the content. Teachers used particular approaches and instructional strategies in service of the content area.

• Ongoing and extensive use of assessment is essential to teaching. Assessment was central to how teachers thought about teaching. They spoke of maintaining a constant focus on how students were responding to lessons and developing an understanding of the material. Informal assessments, in particular, occurred throughout the implementation of lessons and allowed teachers to make rapid adjustments to their lessons in response to student needs.

• Reflection, experience, and pattern recognition are critical. Both of the above points demonstrate aspects of teachers' expertise in recognizing patterns. Teachers used their knowledge and experience to find and respond to patterns in student behavior and learning and to build connections to key patterns within the content areas. Such pattern recognition develops as a result of both formal professional training and experience in the classroom. In reflecting on the ways their teaching had changed over time, teachers frequently alluded—directly and indirectly—to their increased skills of pattern recognition.

教师的想法

TEACHERS' THOUGHTS ON EXPERIENCE, FLEXIBILITY, AND RESPONSIVENESS

China / 中国

"I think my instruction before was rigid and very likely had restricted my students' thinking, but now my instruction is relatively more flexible. I can monitor my students' learning at any time. If they haven't mastered this knowledge point, I immediately associate it with other relevant knowledge points and guide the students to solve the problem. I think the flexibility in my instruction has improved tremendously. I am capable of teaching to the students' characteristics based on their responses in the class."

——————•——————

"This morning, the students . . . indicated that they haven't fully mastered the content. There are always some unpredictable issues or problems that occur during the process of teaching. Sometimes these problems are opportunities for learning growth."

United States / 美国

"Because I've been teaching the same grade for so long, I understand what I'm supposed to teach, and I'm not afraid to let the kids take me off topic and go down a different path. And if I had in my mind that I needed to be their instructor and they needed to adapt to what it is that I want them to learn, then they're not going to learn as much as they can."

——————•——————

"I could see today that we were not done practicing, and that's fine. Tomorrow, I will just delay tomorrow's activity, and we will go back to practicing.

Then, when I feel they are ready—and often they will tell me when they are ready because we are in a partnership—then and only then will they do it independently."

Lessons from the East

As discussed previously, the Chinese teachers demonstrated a more specific structure in their teaching than did the U.S. teachers, yet they demonstrated a clear focus on flexibility within that structure to respond to assessed student needs. They made more use of homework as both an assessment and a reteaching strategy, relying on students' responses to homework to inform changes in their instructional direction or the focus of their lessons. They seemed to place greater value on homework as a tool for learning and assessment than the U.S. teachers did.

They also made specific note of how they used questioning to build from lower-level to higher-level thinking and understanding within lessons, and they paid careful attention to how students responded to those questions to determine whether they could continue the sequence as planned or needed to make adjustments. This skill of listening to what students say and constructing appropriate adaptive responses on a moment-to-moment basis is an exemplary demonstration of teaching expertise (Feiman-Nemser, 2001). Several teachers also described the process of asking students to provide explanations and support to one another as a way of reinforcing learning and responding to areas of need. All of these adjustments, again, were grounded in teachers' ways of thinking about the content and how to support students in their development of content understanding.

> "In these cases, I know it would not work if I keep talking and explaining. But I am sure there must be someone in the class who understands, and I would ask the students to present, demonstrate, and explain to their classmates."

> "I think instruction is a process that requires continuous, new endeavors. There is no rule or silver-bullet strategy; instead, it is a continuously changing process."

Lessons from the West

As discussed in the previous section, teachers in the United States tended to have a student-centered focus in their classrooms, and this was also evident in the ways they demonstrated flexibility. Teachers used assessment of students, including frequent use of authentic assessment, along with their recognition of students' interests and new ideas students brought up to guide potential alterations to their instructional plans. Many teachers commented on the ways they might redirect a lesson or change instructional paths in response to a particular reaction from students:

> "What I envision and what actually happens is rarely the same thing. But I'm very laid-back in that respect, like, 'Well, okay, let's go this direction.'"

———————•———————

> "Well, I think I know exactly what I'm doing, and then in the middle of a lesson we take a turn."

These changes, however, were grounded in the teachers' thorough knowledge of what they were teaching and how they might make adjustments and still maintain the same key goals:

> "In actually teaching the play, I don't have to lay out that I'm going to ask this question and this question, because I probably have 400 questions I could ask depending on how the conversation goes. [I can then] determine the kinds of questions that would be most appropriate for that group and that class."

In addition, teachers described getting a "feel" for the class and lesson and departing from their plans if the atmosphere did not seem conducive to the original outline:

> "I'm also paying attention to where we're at a saturation point. I pay close attention not only in my class but in others, and when everybody's feeling filled with angst and I can just feel them draining, then I'll design some ridiculously easy assignment that we're going to do in class and everybody's going to do well, and all of a sudden everybody is smart again and they are feeling happy again. So a lot of it is understanding who kids are, paying

attention to who they are—constantly adjusting what you're doing."

———•———

"You can pick up on the sense of your class. I remember very specifically one math lesson [where I said], 'I'm having a hard time explaining this to you. None of you seem to understand what I'm saying, so I'm going to stop, we're going to do something completely different, and I'm going to look at this lesson and come up with something different for tomorrow.' So just being able to read your kids, you know . . . and you can read them better if you understand who they are as kids as opposed to just as learners."

Lesson Tool:
Pattern Recognition and Instructional Decision Making

The teachers in our study showed considerable variation in the degree to which their lessons were structured. Many of the teachers in China led highly structured lessons, whereas the U.S. teachers displayed somewhat less structure overall. In both countries, however, teachers discussed being flexible in their practice to allow some change to their instructional plans based on student response. Frequently, they mentioned the degree to which their experience in the classroom informed these decisions and gave them confidence in pursuing alternative pathways within lessons. These comments reflected the concept of pattern recognition, which has been associated with the development of expertise in such diverse fields as chess and diagnostic medicine.

Consider the ways in which pattern recognition is important in classroom practice. When reviewing recorded lessons or visiting peer classrooms, think about the following questions regarding the ebb and flow of the classroom:

- What are the rhythms of classroom behavior?
- What are the shapes and common pathways of instruction and emerging learning?
- What evidence of slight or major detours from the original instructional plan can be seen in the observation?

Then, self-reflect or reflect with a peer on the following questions:

- What prompted the decision to detour?
- How can you describe your "feel" or "sense" of the class?
- What underlying patterns prompted these feelings?

Lesson 4: Attend to Variations in Learners' Needs Through Differentiation

The challenge of responding to the varied needs of all students in any classroom is one that every teacher faces. The teachers in this project provided substantial reflections on their efforts to respond to the range of learners' needs in their classrooms. In part, this was because of specific interview questions that focused on responding to diverse learners' needs, but the theme also emerged throughout teachers' comments across many of the interview questions. In their comments, teachers discussed the varied backgrounds and capabilities for learning they might see within groups of students as well as the range of interests and learning preferences students bring to the classroom. They explained some of the challenges that such a range of needs and preferences might present, along with some of their approaches for and attitudes about responding to those needs. Among the key points that arose in teachers' comments and classroom behaviors related to differentiation were the following:

- There was an emphasis on building multiple pathways to learning through a range of simple and complex differentiation strategies. Teachers talked about some of the simple, more informal approaches they used to support differentiation, and they mentioned some "high-prep" strategies that involve more extensive planning. These pathways included approaches that responded to variations in student readiness and in students' interests and learning preferences.
- Teachers used a variety of grouping formats. They spoke extensively about their approaches to grouping, including their intentions in grouping students by similar abilities or interests in some situations and forming more heterogeneous groups in other instances.
- There was a focus on particular areas of need within the classroom. Many teachers commented on the special needs of particular groups of

learners and explained their concerns about and strategies for working with these groups. The teachers varied considerably in which groups of students they discussed, with some expressing concerns about students who were advanced in their learning, others about students who struggled to reach grade-level expectations and who had identified special needs, and still others about the students "in the middle."

• Most teachers formed foundations for differentiation in assessment. They emphasized the use of formal and informal strategies to determine students' needs for additional support and challenges.

教师的想法
TEACHERS' THOUGHTS ON DIFFERENTIATION

China / 中国

"In such a large class, the individual differences between students are an unavoidable reality, so the teaching has to be individualized. When they enter [class], they have uneven prior learning, so I need to develop and maintain each student's enthusiasm for learning [*xuéxí xìngqù* 学习兴趣], make learning interesting and fun, and cultivate their attitude toward learning English."

"I use a variety of strategies to [differentiate]. For instance, I use after-school time to provide one-to-one tutoring to individual students or tutoring to students in groups. I also give students tiered homework assignments every day based on their needs and learning abilities. Because you cannot pay attention to all students within the limited instructional time, you have to come up with other complementary means."

United States / 美国

"I've thought about this often, and I believe honestly that every student is a special needs student. Every single one of them has something special, some special need. I think they are all important."

"I look to see whether I am making it rigorous or hard for them. I tell students throughout the building that my job is to make their brains hurt, because if your brain isn't struggling, it's not growing. So if it's too easy, then I'm not doing my job."

Lessons from the East

For the teachers in China, differentiation tended to be about directing more advanced questions and activities to more advanced learners. It was also about providing greater direct support and tutoring to students who were struggling. Teachers spoke often of using tiered assignments and tiered questioning to present students with tasks at different levels of demand. Another strategy that teachers spoke of using frequently was a peer tutoring/peer support approach, whereby they would link students who had demonstrated mastery of particular content with their peers who were struggling. Teachers also employed additional tutoring approaches beyond class time to support students who were struggling with a particular concept or lesson.

"The curriculum illustrates the basic learning objectives and more advanced levels of learning as well. I would do tiered instruction—only ask advanced learners to tackle advanced learning problems. For students of lower levels of learning abilities, I usually find they can solve some of the advanced problems as well after receiving my instruction."

"I would ask students of different learning abilities to answer different levels of questions, so that every student can experience success [*chéngjiùgǎn* 成就感] in the classroom."

"If the feedback indicates a certain student is having problems with the content on that day. I would ask the student to stay a little bit longer and address his learning problems. Maybe a few days later, there might be another student running into learning problems. So the tutoring is flexible."

One of the key organizational differences between U.S. and Chinese schools was class size, and this seemed to have a strong relationship with how teachers thought about differentiation. The large class sizes in China, combined with a high density of curriculum content, were associated with the teachers' extensive use of whole-group instruction, lectures, and strategies in which students were asked to help one another.

> "I hope that I can teach a class having a size of 30 students. That would be ideal. Currently, my class has more than 50 students, and I used to have classes of more than 60 students. They do have uneven learning abilities. . . . I really think there are certain restraints in improving their learning, but that is not something we have influence on."

> "However, large class size has an advantage—it's easier to take advantage of the peer/group influence among the students themselves. When students are in a bigger collective group [*jítǐ* 集体], they are more likely to have a sense of belonging—each student feels that he or she is a member of this collective group."

These whole-group instructional activities are somewhat less conducive to differentiation than approaches that make use of small-group work, for example. Nevertheless, teachers embedded some tiered questioning within their whole-group instruction, and they emphasized how they were using assessment approaches to note students' progress and encourage tutoring and practice for struggling students.

Lessons from the West

Teachers in the United States placed a strong emphasis on responding to students' differences and promoting access for all students to educational experiences that would respond to their individual needs. Their comments and practices clearly reflected trends in U.S. education that focus on inclusion and appropriately differentiated responses to academic and cultural diversity in classrooms (Tomlinson et al., 2003). In their efforts to accomplish these goals of differentiated and responsive practice, the teachers made extensive use of varied grouping practices that allow students to work on different tasks at different paces, and they used a variety of materials to engage and challenge their students.

Much of the discussion surrounding differentiation focused on students who brought different levels of ability, background knowledge, and other aspects of readiness for learning to the classroom. Individual teachers talked about some of the specific challenges they faced and efforts they made to support particular groups of students. Some spoke more extensively about students with identified special needs in their classrooms and how they worked to respond to these learners, whereas others emphasized the difficulty of ensuring ongoing challenge and engagement for more advanced learners who tended to reach understanding more quickly than their classmates.

> "In my classroom, I find that it's easier to work with students who are more challenged than the ones who get it super fast. It's hard to keep those kids engaged. They get the answers so fast, so when I come in with four or five things to do, that's 20 minutes for them, and for everybody else it might be three classes."

———————•———————

> "Oftentimes, I'm not as concerned about the kids who are at the top and the kids who are at the bottom because they have extra people looking out for them. It's those kids in the middle who are incredibly capable but have either low opinions of self-worth, or they just don't feel comfortable in a large-group situation, and they just need to be able to feel comfortable to be able to open up and blossom. So I find ways to make them speak publicly, or I find ways for them to find pleasure in doing something with a small group so they can build more confidence instead of being in the background. Worrying about that group in the middle, I think, is equally as important as at both ends."

Beyond these emphases on differences in readiness, teachers also talked about the importance of responding to differences in students' interests and learning preferences in order to promote learning. They noted the value of incorporating students' interests into instruction and recognizing when tailoring instruction toward students' preferred ways of learning was conducive to growth and when they needed to guide students toward taking risks outside their comfort zones.

> "The other thing is I try to remember is to involve them all even when they want to be invisible. They think they want to be invisible, so I had this little deal where I'll have Monday, Tuesday, Wednesday, Thursday, and Friday kids. If it's Tuesday, then my Tuesday kids are going to get a question. You'd think they'd figure this out, but they never do."

Just as the Chinese teachers spoke of assessing which students might need tutoring on particular content at any given time, the U.S. teachers also discussed instances of providing special, individualized support to respond to students' needs, as in the following example:

> "I have one student who was writing absolutely nothing for me. And after about three or four weeks, I cornered him in the hall and said, 'Look. There are three reasons and three reasons only why students don't write in English. These are the three reasons, so which one are you?' He said, 'This is the one—I don't know how to get started.' And I had him come in after school on Friday so we could sit down and I could show him how to get started. For two hours, that kid sat next to me. I sat at the computer and asked questions. I typed up his responses in outline form and did half of the essay. I handed it to him and said, 'Do you understand it now?' He said he did, and that child has not missed an essay since."

Practical Tips: Recognizing the Differentiation and Assessment Connection

The following tips are explained in further detail by Tomlinson and Imbeau (2010) and Wormeli (2006):

- Recognize the integral and critical relationship between differentiation and assessment. Differentiation must be driven by assessment, because instruction that is responsive to students' needs and differences must be informed by the methods we use to learn about those needs and differences.

• Develop and use preassessment strategies consistently. Preassessment provides evidence regarding (1) what students already know about upcoming instruction; (2) the degree to which students are prepared to start the upcoming instruction; and (3) what upcoming instruction can be eliminated or should be supplemented and for which students.

• Use ongoing assessment—both formal and informal—to support adjustments in the instructional plan that respond to students' progress and pace of learning.

• Employ multiple forms of assessment that allow students to demonstrate their learning in ways that are appropriate not only to the content area but also, when possible, to students' individual learning preferences.

• Clarify for students and parents the distinctions between assessment and grading.

Lesson Tool:
Analyzing Differentiated Tasks

Some lessons and tasks incorporate "low-prep" differentiation, which involves making small adjustments to prepare for and respond to student differences. Others may be described as incorporating "high-prep" differentiation, which usually means selecting or developing various versions of tasks, stimuli, or student support materials to address students' needs. Tiered tasks, which were noted frequently by the Chinese teachers, are a form of high-prep differentiation that involves multiple versions of a task or activity. These versions represent different degrees of complexity and challenge, and they are presented to different students based on their assessed levels of readiness. Tiered tasks usually focus on similar learning outcomes but through different pathways, which provide additional support and scaffolding to some students while presenting less repetition and additional challenge to other students. An additional benefit of tiered tasks is that, if properly designed, they may engage students for similar amounts of time regardless of their level of readiness. This is because the tasks are tailored to respond to groups of students that represent different levels. Some curricular materials present tasks that are already tiered or easily lend themselves to tiering. Teachers may also construct tiered tasks by building an initial activity and then adjusting it to construct several variations.

Some of the key differences among tiered tasks may be simple versus complex, concrete versus abstract, or foundational versus transformational. Alternatively, the differences may emerge around such elements as the level of structure provided or the level of independence allowed. Tomlinson (1999, 2001) has identified multiple considerations for teachers and curriculum developers as they think about the types of adjustments that are necessary while building or selecting tiered tasks. Critical among these is ensuring that all versions of a task are respectful and meaningful and that the differences among versions are not limited to quantity (i.e., tiered tasks should avoid "busywork" practice for students who finish quickly).

In reviewing or constructing tiered tasks for use with students at varying levels of readiness, consider questions such as the following to evaluate your activities:

- What is it that makes the activities at different levels similar to one another? What features do they all share?
- How are the activities different? What makes one version of a task more appropriate for an advanced learner or more appropriate for a struggling learner?
- How fully do all of the activities address the same or related objectives? How do the assessment processes relate?

Lesson 5: Be Mindful of Your Instruction, Content, and Learning Environment

The work of the teachers in our project reflected an intense focus on creating and maintaining a safe, fun, and intellectually stimulating learning environment—which works as an umbrella over the entirety of this book. The learning environment is a reflection of the teacher as a person and of the planning involved in preparing for teaching. Furthermore, the construction of a learning environment and a teacher's approach to the management of that environment are integrally related. However, it is also important to include the learning environment as a key theme in our discussion of instructional delivery. Key findings from our observations and interviews about the learning environment included the following points:

- An awareness of students' needs is influential to instruction. Not only did teachers use assessment, as mentioned previously, to ensure that students were academically ready for the tasks in which they engaged; they also considered students' emotional and behavioral readiness for the instruction. Teachers then made necessary modifications to promote students' focus on learning or to respond to other, more immediately pressing needs.

- A sense of safety is a foundation for learning. Consciously or unconsciously, implicitly or explicitly, the teachers demonstrated the value they placed on students' sense of safety as a prerequisite for learning. They regularly commented on building an environment in which students could feel safe to take risks, share their ideas, and make mistakes in the service of learning and growing. Related to this sense of safety was a sense that teachers were promoting a learning community within their classrooms and encouraging students to support one another in striving toward learning and growth.

- The use of physical space can serve instructional purposes. The teachers were thoughtful about how they organized their physical space to support instructional purposes. They had various amounts of flexibility and control over their physical space, yet they made conscious choices about how they used that space to support learning.

教师的想法

TEACHERS' THOUGHTS ON AN ENVIRONMENT
CONDUCIVE TO LEARNING

China / 中国

"My classroom is very casual and informal. The students don't have to sit at their seats all the time. They can walk around. And they can do whatever they want to, as long as it is conducive to learning."

"As a mathematics teacher, I hope that my classroom is a dynamic learning environment, which means that the mathematics classroom should be a training ground for the development of thinking skills and problem-solving skills, where students can play their thinking capacities to their fullest, where they can take risks and make wild connections, and where they can expand their horizons of thinking."

United States / 美国

"Kids feel very free to ask for help because we create a very safe environment. I love the fact that today there were three different opinions about what the thesis statement was . . . and one girl didn't back down because it's safe to be the only one in the room. I work hard. There is no making fun because someone disagrees. Sometimes, I have them line up on opposites sides of the room and allow them to convince each other and allow people to swap places if they like. We are here to explore ideas. The kids today were not looking for the right answer from the teacher. That's the environment I want—that it's safe to explore ideas and it's safe to change your mind."

Lessons from the East

The learning environment in the Chinese classrooms we observed, as noted, tended to reflect a greater use of whole-class instruction, lectures, and structures than the U.S. classrooms. Teachers also had less flexibility with their physical space in Chinese classrooms, in part because of their large class sizes. Furthermore, teachers in China demonstrated an emphasis on control and authority (*wēiyán* 威严) within the learning environment, reflecting a more pronounced hierarchical structure. However, the teachers also demonstrated a specific and conscientious focus on students' needs within the learning environment and on providing ways to ensure that the environment was conducive to learning. Several notable comments emerged from our interviews that demonstrate an emphasis on communicating a sense of safety and respect to students:

> "In my teaching, I try to avoid things that would hurt the students. For instance, our lesson today was about composition. I would not ask them specifically to write about their mother

or their father, because I know that some students come from single-parent families; that would hurt their feelings."

In addition, teachers' comments reflected an emphasis on building an environment in which the students felt a sense of community, through which they celebrated and supported one another's efforts to succeed in instructional activities:

"Some of the students have better English learning abilities. . . . I would call one of these high-performing students to answer my questions; they will give the correct answer. Then I will ask the whole class to give a round of applause, so that students can see some classmates are ahead of them in learning and thereby will have more enthusiasm for learning."

———————•———————

"Occasionally, I select a student to stand and recite a response. Once the student gives his or her answer, the rest of the students clap and immediately proceed with the next math problem."

Throughout their comments, the teachers consistently maintained a focus on content and learning, thus demonstrating the degree to which the general learning environment and the specifics of instruction were integrally related:

"For instance, during the afternoon classes, the students often feel tired—especially when they do not have a nice break during lunch. In these cases, if the teacher can tell some jokes, that could liven up the climate [*diàodòng qìfen* 调动气氛]. Also, the jokes should relate to the learning content."

Lessons from the West

U.S. teachers generally had more flexibility in how they used their physical classroom space. They tended more often to physically organize their students into groups for instruction and to make frequent changes to the classroom setup to support the relevant instructional strategy being implemented. Teachers commented on making the classroom environment a welcoming space—one designed to provide learning stimuli and to allow active, busy participation:

> "It has to be an inviting space. The things that are up have to be relevant to what students are learning. I use them a lot as tools in teaching. [For example], these are all words that my 3rd graders got when we read *The Phantom Tollbooth*."

———•———

> "Some activities I want to do are kind of loud just by nature. They are kind of noisy. It's productive work, but it's noisy."

Like their Chinese counterparts, U.S. teachers also emphasized creating a safe environment for risk taking:

> "I want it to be a classroom where they feel welcome, so I have to create that welcoming environment and create that atmosphere where they feel relaxed, where they are not afraid to say something silly. They know I'm going to reward them for what they do well rather than be punitive so that they are not afraid to take a chance."

Lesson Tool:
Being Invitational

Several of the lesson tools in this chapter suggested ways of reflecting on instructional practice by analyzing the content and procedures involved in lessons. This tool encourages reviewing lessons for the degree to which they invite and encourage students. Just as we can classify our questions to students based on cognitive level or whether they are open- or closed-ended, we can also classify our questions and directions to students based on how inviting the learning environment is.

Costa (2001) emphasized the importance of asking questions that are invitational. In other words, the form of a question might suggest that multiple responses are possible, or the wording might include words that indicate when tentative or "risky" responses are acceptable. Wragg and Brown (2001) distinguished between questions that are encouraging and those that are threatening in tone and format. Walsh and Sattes (2005) explored ways a teacher might ensure that more students have an opportunity to be involved in questioning and discussion. Suggested approaches include more teacher movement around the classroom, frequent seat changes for students, and use of directed questions (posed to specific students) and undirected questions (posed to the class for volunteers to answer) in equal measure.

Similar to the lesson review suggested around types of questions earlier in this chapter, record a lesson and then go back and review all of the questions asked and directions given. Rate each question or direction according to some of the elements noted above. For example, classify each question, direction, or follow-up on a student's answer as encouraging or threatening; rate how invitational the questions sound; count how many times specific students participate and note how many never participate at all; or measure how much wait time is given in which students might respond or continue an answer. Then, given the results, select a dimension for growth in future lessons and continue to record and analyze the patterns of invitation within the classroom.

The flowchart in Figure 4.5 provides an example of how to capture the flow of questioning during a lesson. Simply map out your seating arrangement and ask a colleague to draw arrows that show the flow of questioning during a 10-minute time span. In the example depicted in Figure 4.5, five questions were asked: three from teacher to student, one from student to teacher, and one from student to student. Another interesting finding in this example is that one side of the classroom was not involved in the questioning at all.

Summary

Teachers play many roles in schools and classrooms, but at the center of those diverse roles is the responsibility for facilitating student learning through classroom instruction. The teachers we interviewed and observed in the United States and China demonstrated their instructional skills across a wide array of grade levels and content areas, and they represented a range of styles and preferences in how they presented material and involved their students in the learning process. Yet across the group, the teachers demonstrated facility with implementing multiple activities

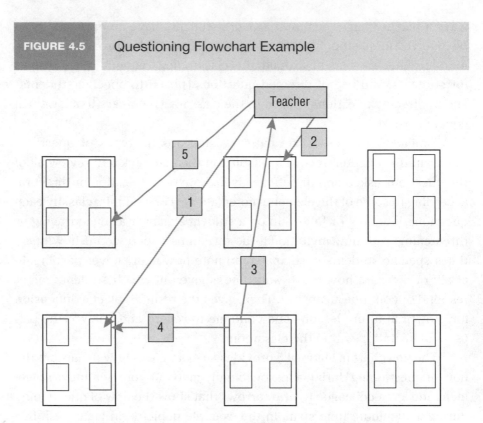

FIGURE 4.5 Questioning Flowchart Example

during lessons, keeping students engaged, responding and adjusting to varied student needs and classroom circumstances, and ensuring an environment centered around learning. The teachers showed confidence in their instruction and habits of critical reflection by acknowledging the ways that their experience informed their decision making and the ways in which they might seek to develop particular instructional skills further. Among all the teachers, high levels of student engagement and an emphasis on the dynamic interaction between their teaching decisions and evidence of student learning are sure signs of the expertise and talent represented in the group.

5

Classroom Organization, Management, and Discipline

第五章：课堂组织，管理和纪律

These experiences [during my early years of teaching] were very helpful, which made me aware that the key to successful classroom instruction is classroom management and organization. —Chinese teacher

As a new teacher, I started off trying to get behavior management down. That was the challenge. I learned to collaborate more with other teachers who have more expertise that I don't. I've found the line between nice and demanding. —U.S. teacher

Working with preservice teachers, classroom management is often an area for which they want more training and with which they struggle the most when beginning to teach. When asked about classroom management through the lens of a KWL (know, want to learn, learned) format, the responses are consistent. They *know* the importance of classroom management and *want to know* how to do it, including how to find the right balance (e.g., individual versus group needs, structure and flexibility, kindness and firmness). Explicit instruction in classroom management is a relatively new addition to courses in schools of education; teachers trained in the 1970s and 1980s were unlikely to have had a management class. Classroom management was seen as a skill developed from experience.

> "My high school had pre-internship for teachers (visiting a classroom). My college had practica every semester. When I graduated, I had experience in grades 1–8. I could anticipate what students would do because I had experienced it. (This was most influential.)" *(United States)*

———•———

> "Especially at the early stage of my teaching career, I often felt confused. One of the biggest challenges I had was that my students did not listen to me and had all sorts of off-task behaviors. Some students even drove me to tears. I even told my parents that I didn't want to be a teacher anymore. That was a painful and difficult period of time. However, through continuous reflection and learning, I survived. There were a number of experienced teachers there by my side who supported me. That meant a lot to me." *(China)*

Today, there has been an explosion in the number of texts on classroom management in the United States, but academic courses remain fairly limited. Texts on the subject in China have just begun to appear over the past few years. A combination of coursework and practice are needed for new teachers to begin to master such skills. It's been shown that teachers make over 1,000 decisions each day (Kauchak & Eggen, 2013), so they must have sufficient practice in order to develop a repertoire of nearly automatic responses to situations if they want to successfully manage a classroom. Once this occurs, classroom management seems almost intuitive.

Ironically, even though it's a critical skill, it takes a backseat in daily classroom activities. According to one Chinese teacher:

> "There has been a significant change in my teaching methods. Before, I sought to make teaching methods distinctive from one

another. I have a clear list of instructional methods—number one is this, number two is that, and number three is that. Gradually, I started to realize that the best teaching is markless/traceless."

Observation in the classrooms we visited supported the existence of strong classroom organization, management, and discipline. Overall, though, the teachers' interviews offered more insight into their beliefs about students and management. Like many aspects of excellent teaching, when classroom management is executed effectively, it is not obvious and is seamlessly woven into the lesson. A nonpractitioner might realize that a lesson went smoothly but would have no clear understanding of *why*. By contrast, fellow teachers—with explicit knowledge of management basics—are able to identify the structure and nuances that an expert teacher brings to the classroom. Classroom management can be considered to be the underpinning for successful instruction, and it supports and is supported by all of the factors discussed in previous chapters. Therefore, some of the discussion in this chapter will repeat themes identified previously but within a slightly different context.

So, what did our teachers teach us about classroom organization, management, and discipline? Two particularly interesting findings are the high number of instructional activities incorporated into a single 40- to 60-minute lesson (averaging 9–10 activities) and the high level of student engagement. The connection should be obvious: engagement is kept high by shifting activities frequently. In this way, students don't have an opportunity to become disengaged, and it is easier for teachers to reach students with different learning preferences. But how do you make this process seamless or traceless (*wúhén* 无痕)? There must be skilled classroom management operating in the background.

Using very simple definitions of *culture* and *climate* can be a framework for exploring classroom management. Deal and Kennedy (2000) define culture as "the way we do things around here." Applied to a classroom, the rules, expectations, procedures, and routines of the classroom comprise a great deal of a classroom's culture. If climate is defined as "the way we feel about the way we do things around here," then *how* rules, expectations, procedures, and routines are developed, introduced, and reinforced within the classroom would certainly influence the way a classroom "feels." The teachers who invited us into their classrooms were masters at creating welcoming, safe environments that reduced the likelihood of misbehavior and increased the chances for student success.

- Climate: the technical approach to how things are done in class
  - Effectively using *available resources*
  - Maintaining *high levels of student engagement* during lessons
- Culture: the affective sense of belonging and safety in the classroom
  - Engaging in *positive discipline*
  - Developing *respectful relationships*

--- 教室聚光灯 ---

CLASSROOM SPOTLIGHT

Physical arrangement of the classroom is a component of classroom management. A teacher's ability to influence the arrangement is affected by resources, including space. Teachers often lament the restrictions of their environment. Large class sizes in China limit opportunities for creative arrangements. Therefore, orderly rows facing the front of the room has been the most pervasive method of classroom organization. Furthermore, classroom decorations are sparse and usually consist of several posters or banners.

In a middle school classroom in China's Yunnan Province, there were 72 first-year students, which is a typical size for this region of the country. The desks were arranged in five rows of two, and the class was almost evenly divided between girls and boys. We were told that the students didn't yet know one another well. They had only been in school for 12 days since we visited at the start of a new school year. The students came from 11 or 12 separate primary schools, including at least one mountain (rural) school. There were approximately 2,100 students and 110 teachers in the school. The primary decorations in the classroom were large red and yellow posters hanging on the front wall, which read "Self-respect," "Confidence," "Make yourself strong," "Be independent," and "Self-esteem."

There was more variety in the physical arrangement of classrooms in the United States. Larger rooms, more equipment, and many more decorative elements were evident. As an example, a 3rd grade U.S. classroom had 23 students: 12 boys and 11 girls. Some students lived in multi-million-dollar homes and others lived in inexpensive hotels. The total number of students was 20 at the start of the year; several have already left and been replaced by new students. One student enrolled just a week ago. The students' desks were arranged in groups of four since the teacher frequently used cooperative learning. Three extra tables flanked students' desks for small-group work, including work with the special education teacher and her paraeducator. The TV was mounted high in one corner, and there was a microwave on the back counter where students who had not eaten breakfast could make instant oatmeal. Student work and posters with Kagan cooperative group activities were displayed on the walls, and the whiteboard at the front of the room listed the day's agenda and assignments for different reading and math groups.

Lesson 1: Use Available Resources Effectively

Teachers in both countries identified the benefits and challenges of different resources available to support their teaching. They believed it was their responsibility to be as effective and efficient as possible with those resources to meet the needs of their students and the outside pressures that shaped the content to be covered. Human resources, time resources, and physical resources all came into play in the instructional decisions each teacher made.

—————— 教师的想法 ——————

TEACHERS' THOUGHTS ON THE USE OF RESOURCES

China / 中国

"When I teach mathematics, I use the windows, ceiling, and roof to teach geometric shapes."

"When I prepare my teaching, I prepare the materials I will use. When I prepare my lesson, I prepare how to explain things, what I will say to explain the lesson. Also, I will prepare the procedures for the class."

———•———

"Teachers in China have to make sure that students master certain learning objectives in 40 minutes—the length of the lesson. That's why the classroom has to be very productive in the time slot we [have available] to accomplish this. So, the learning objective is highly focused in the lesson, and it's very consistent."

———•———

"Yes, in China, we do have larger class sizes. There is indeed a need to encourage and mobilize [*diàodòng* 调动] students in the classroom. Therefore, in my own classroom, I try to encourage, mobilize, and praise my students and use feedback to lead students to be immersed in the poetic setting."

United States / 美国

"I try to keep it pretty clutter-free; I try to keep a lot of room between the tables. I try to have groups that function well together; I might have to move people around a little bit. I'm kind of always playing around with things. Kind of colorful but not overwhelming."

———•———

"First thing is the way the room is set up. My class is so huge that ideally they would all be looking at each other all the time. But I just have too many kids, which is another thing—I started out with 12 in 2000 and now I start with 42."

———•———

"When I have shorter time frames and when I did 5th grade—when I had to lecture—it was more of a show because I would have to get that information across to them before we could do the experiment the next time. Because our sessions were short, I presented [material] in different ways and had students interact with me during the lecture so it wasn't straight, strict, 'Sit there and listen to me for half an hour.' It's more like, 'You interact with me for half an hour, but I'm still doing most of the talking.'"

Time was a common challenge among our teachers. Given the limits of time, it was imperative that they protect their instructional time with effective time management. Clear expectations for behavior (rules) and established procedures and routines (the backbone of classroom management) provide teachers with more time to teach (Goor, Schwenn, & Goor, 1997; Wong & Wong, 2009). Differences were evident in class size and physical resources. Teachers in the United States had fewer students per class, more resources (including access to technology), and more physical space than their counterparts in China.

Lesson from the East

The number of students in typical Chinese classes affects the options available for physical arrangement. There is no room for many of the "extras" we expect to see in U.S. classrooms. There is no space for extra tables, reading corners, and so on. Though technology and software, such as PowerPoint, is available in more schools than ever before, schools outside large urban areas have a much more limited access to such resources. For example, one of our teachers moved his physics class to the auditorium for our visit since it was the only venue in the school with an LCD projector, which he needed for the lesson. The teachers, however, were very adept at finding ways to reframe what many in the West might consider limitations and using them to their benefit. Even large classes could be seen as beneficial, as is evident in the following teacher's comment:

> "However, large class size has an advantage—it's easier to take advantage of the peer/group influence among the students themselves. When students are in a bigger collective group, they are more likely to have a sense of belonging—each student feels that he or she is a member of this collective group. . . . Also, a larger class size has another advantage: there are more resources to share among the students. Different students come from different backgrounds and bring with them different resources. These resources can be complementary. But on the other hand, a large class size also has many disadvantages. For instance, I try my best to encourage every single student in my class to participate; however, I cannot guarantee that all students have an opportunity to

present themselves. Therefore, I strive to build in more activities (such as pair or group activities) that allow every student to have the opportunity to contribute."

The physics teacher mentioned earlier used common objects for his experiments and had the students provide them:

"For instance, today, I didn't prepare the materials needed for the experiment. The students brought them. Those materials are readily accessible in their daily life. The students know how to deal with them, and I don't need to teach them. They can do the experiment when they get home. Some students were not able to finish the experiment in class, but they can continue to finish it when they get home. For instance, when we talked about the experiment with the windmill today, the light was too strong and the picture on the screen did not show up well. When the students get home tonight, they can use that set of materials to make their own windmill."

Though the limit of class time was a challenge, teachers made it an opportunity to create highly focused lessons. As noted in Chapter 3, teachers in China generally have larger classes, but they teach fewer classes and have more time to plan targeted lessons. One teacher even made the time limit a motivational strategy in her class:

"Anyway, whenever I step into the class, my students can see the anxious look on my face. I would say, 'Students, hurry up! The time is sneaking away and it is not waiting for you. We have a lot to cover in the next 45 minutes. The bell is going to ring before you know it.' I would share my anxiety intentionally in every class. When the students feel my eagerness, they cheer up, concentrate on learning, and pay attention."

Teachers noted the importance of procedures and routines to the effective use of time and smooth flow of lessons:

"This is a habit that the students and the teacher formed over a long period of time. For example, in a class with so many kids, we set up a few basic requirements: when it is time to discuss, you should participate and express your point of view; when it is your turn to speak, you should speak boldly and illustrate your point; when it is time to listen quietly, you must calm down and listen. These are the requirements at the school level, too. We expect our kids to form these positive learning habits over time."

Lessons from the West

Teachers in the United States often had more classroom space for the number of students in each class and were able to incorporate a variety of physical resources—from additional furniture to technology. They shared many more comments about the ways in which they used the classroom space and spent more time rearranging that space to meet the interests of their students and the needs of the lesson.

"The classroom arrangement is so that students look at each other and you can't hide. You can't hide in my classroom anywhere. You are visible all the time by the teacher. I see all those kids."

"I make it interesting. The stuff I put up is relevant to whatever we're talking about. I make it a cool place, so they're like, 'Yeah, I wanna be in there.' The students were telling [a new student], 'Wait until you get into her room; she has Tiggers everywhere!' It has to be an inviting space. The things that are up have to be relevant to what they're learning. I use them a lot as tools in teaching."

"I try to make it as kid-friendly as I can. I put kid work out in the hall, but in the classroom I try to put up learning poster kind of stuff, but it's still very kid-oriented."

"It's very fluid. . . . Even in my regular class when I was a classroom teacher, I was constantly moving things out of the way so that I could use the floor space. The kids knew just because it's here now doesn't mean it's going to be here tomorrow. This afternoon, the tables will be all around the circle so that we can continue with our circle class."

In some ways, this extra space creates its own challenges for the teachers.

"It's just trying to find different space for the different things—I run out of space!"

———————•———————

"I'd like to work on my orderliness, but I'm having a hard time balancing creativity and orderliness. And if you guys can find that perfect balance, please let me know . . . if you find somebody, I'd like to go to visit them!"

U.S. teachers expressed their sense of time differently than their Chinese counterparts did. They noted the role of classroom management in saving instructional time:

"Well, I try to have a lot of class management things in place so that a lot of time isn't spent on class management. All the rules are in Japanese and they know them, so I'm able to say things like 'Sit down,' 'Don't touch that'—a lot of those things I can say in Japanese."

Although there was reference to meeting standards and a packed curriculum, many teachers expressed the importance of using time to go beyond the mandates of the curriculum.

"I often pair a new student with a friendly helper. You have to stop instruction to make the transition as peaceful and comfortable as possible. Take time to introduce the child to the class and explain routines. It's a big deal for the child."

———————•———————

"[Teaching the whole child] is something that's really important to me. . . . I've put it above everything else. I try to create a community with my kids. You know, what research is showing is that a lot of the reason for the violence is because they don't feel connected. So we take our 40 minutes every morning to do our connections."

Because many U.S. classrooms have relatively few students, teachers are able to focus on individual needs:

"I'm kind of focused on . . . what's each kid doing and how can you tweak your plans, lessons, and management to teach individual kids?"

"As the year has progressed, we've seen these students trust us, and I targeted three students as a litmus test to see about my own success as their teacher. They were the three kids most allergic to writing, and one just practically breaks out in hives every time he takes out a pen to write anything. I try to get to know that kid through the year as a person and as a learner and to find what it is that interests that child and to find those avenues that get him engaged."

"I guess the thing that was important is the fact that I have rigorous standards but am able to create a classroom where every child feels like he or she is the most important person in the room."

Whether or not the teachers identified specific management elements in their interviews, they met common standards for effective management of resources. In their classrooms, they made sure they could see their students and their students could see them. They made sure there was access to walk around the classroom, they had all the materials for the lesson at hand and did not spend priceless instructional time looking for a handout, a book, or student materials. The expectations (rules) and procedures made it possible for teachers to shift easily from one activity to another without losing time to direct students in a process that they already knew.

Teachers used the resource of time to meet students' individual needs. In the larger Chinese classes, teachers were able to work with students in tutoring sessions and after school. Although some U.S. teachers made time after school to work with individual students, they discussed it much less. However, longer instructional blocks and smaller classes allowed teachers to use their instructional time to meet such needs.

Lesson Tool: Systematic Teaching of Procedures

Effective teachers are masters at teaching and maintaining procedures within their classrooms. Think about all of the repeated processes your students must complete each day. Do you have a systematic way to complete these activities? Do your students know the processes and do they follow them? Here are a few common procedures that will be found in most teachers' classrooms (Evertson & Emmer, 2013):

- Asking for assistance
- Pencil sharpening
- Using the restroom
- Entering the classroom
- Dismissal
- Practicing fire drills and other emergency drills
- Handing in work
- Distributing materials

Once you have identified your main procedures, write out the specific steps needed to accomplish each task. During the first weeks of the school year, take the time to teach these procedures explicitly to your class. Your written lists of steps can be shared with coteachers, substitute teachers, and students who arrive after the year has begun. Procedures should be taught explicitly. When students have mastered the procedures, you will spend less time on management and have more time to provide meaningful instruction.

The following are steps for the direct instruction of procedures:

- Describe and demonstrate the desired behavior.
  - Give the context. When will students use the procedure?

- Give the rationale. Why should students follow the procedure? What is the benefit?
- Model. Act out the steps of the procedures for students.
• Rehearse the procedure.
- Have students practice the procedure as a role-play. *(simulated)*
- Give students the opportunity to practice in an actual situation while providing guidance, as needed. Keep practicing until students have mastered the procedures. *(guided practice)*
- Once mastered, review and practice as needed (e.g., when students are beginning to forget steps or around special holidays that affect class routines). *(distributed)*
• Provide ongoing feedback.
- Correct and redirect errors in steps. Continue to practice.
- Praise accurate completion of the task. Avoid generalized statements, and identify what students have done specifically.

教室聚光灯

CLASSROOM SPOTLIGHT

Despite the different resources available and physical arrangement limitations, teachers in both countries maintain high levels of student engagement. Use of multiple instructional arrangements, including whole-class, small-group, and individual work within one lesson, was a common feature across classrooms.

There are 72 junior middle school students in the Chinese class introduced at the beginning of this chapter. During our observation, the students rose in unison, bowed, and recited a welcome when class began. The teacher wrote instructions on the chalkboard (no other instructional equipment was in the room). When instructed, the students all turned to their backpacks, took out their notepads and pencils, and began working on the math problems written on the board. We observed not a single off-task behavior. Once the students began the algebra equations, the teacher circulated among the students and occasionally stopped to whisper a word or look over a student's shoulder. After 5–10 minutes, he gave additional instructions, and the students began comparing their work in small groups of four. After a few more minutes, the teacher returned to the chalkboard and began asking the students to solve the equations. The students then called out in oral recitation the answers to his questions and the answers to the math problems.

Lesson 2: Maintain High Levels of Student Engagement

While observing teachers, we monitored their classes for student engagement after every five minutes of activity and used a three-point scale to identify the level of engagement. At the high end of the scale was a 3, which translated to at least 80 percent of the class appearing to be participating appropriately. The average for U.S. teachers was 2.6, and Chinese teachers averaged 2.9—both of which indicated high levels of student engagement. As mentioned earlier in this chapter, the teachers averaged 9–10 activities per instructional period observed, partially explaining these high levels of engagement. The classroom management skills that allowed these teachers to smoothly transition from one activity to another—a well-organized class, prepared and accessible materials, and established expectations and procedures—were discussed in the first lesson. There are three additional classroom management elements seen among the teachers in our study that support on-task behavior. The teachers used proximity control (walking among students while conducting a lesson to reduce distance and reinforce awareness of the students' behavior), a variety of grouping arrangements, and strategic ways to monitor students.

―――――――――― 教师的想法 ――――――――――

TEACHERS' THOUGHTS ON STUDENT ENGAGEMENT

China / 中国

"I usually walk around the classroom during teaching."

――――――――

"In addition, before the lesson starts, I memorize five students' names and call them during the lesson. This is really important. When you call students by their names, they know that the teacher is paying attention to them."

———•———

"I walked around a lot, interacting with my students. I'm really doing the troubleshooting as well. I get close to the students, and in group learning, the groups are formed based on students' learning abilities. So in pairs there is one who is advanced and one who is less advanced. I know my students' prior learning really well, so I know what to look for when I walk around."

———•———

"We are now implementing the teaching strategy of student grouping. There are 12 learning groups in my class. Each group is heterogeneous, consisting of both high-performing and low-performing students."

———•———

"It is challenging for teachers to take care of all of the students. So I adopted the approach of grouping for learning, in which the students are partners and can learn from each other."

United States / 美国

"The other [important] thing during the class is proximity. Although I begin my instruction standing at the front of the room, I do circulate, and so does Mr. O. We are always with all the kids."

———•———

"I try to maintain eye contact as much as possible. I don't focus straight ahead. I turn my body. I want them to know 'I'm looking at you, too.' And I think they know that by now—just walking around and checking on their work. When the kids are there, I'm on. And that really helps a lot with keeping kids on task."

———•———

"I try to do a lot of high student engagement; I get the students up and around. I model new skills, using the overhead and examples and then have the students complete independent practice. I use a lot of cooperative learning to increase on-task behavior. I incorporate games, cheering, and chanting. Active learning will increase their learning. I'm constantly assessing; they don't even know who I'm watching."

Research has shown that high levels of student engagement and student achievement are linked (Jones, 2009; Klem & Connell, 2004), and these teachers worked intentionally to include all of their students in meaningful lessons that capture the students' attention and maintain their focus.

Lesson from the East

During our observations, the Chinese teachers moved through their classrooms, but they did not mention this in their interviews unless we asked them about it specifically. They were more likely to discuss having their students move around as a means of increasing attention to and engagement with the lesson. It seems likely that this is related to the recent educational reforms in China. Traditionally, teachers may move around the classroom, but having the students move is still a novel approach in the classroom. Nevertheless, it's one that they found useful.

Group work is another recent addition to their repertoire. The teachers were able to effectively shift from mini-lecture to small-group work to whole-group discussions because their students had mastered the necessary procedures. Groups were intentionally formed to be heterogeneous. Grouping by skill or interest level was not observed. Furthermore, cooperative grouping is consistent with the Chinese emphasis on community. Given the number of students in each classroom, teachers identified grouping as a way to increase the active engagement of more students.

> "The way we do student grouping is more likely in the form of peer tutoring [*hùzhù xiǎozǔ* 互助小组]. Each group has some high-performing, average-performing, and low-performing students, so the students can cooperate with, support, and learn from one another."

"One way [to maintain students' participation] is to have cooperative student learning. Every student has his or her responsibility assigned."

––––––•––––––

"Sometimes, when I just stand there and do the lecturing, students have a hard time understanding me; however, when I ask students to explain in their own words [by working in groups], their peers understand better."

––––––•––––––

"I started using hands-on activities (experiments) only two years ago. When I take over a class of students, I divide the class into groups and select one student as a leader for each group. The leader should have certain skills in organizational management. Each group will learn different content. . . . For instance, in the lesson you observed, one group used origami and folded little planes, and one group used a ping-pong ball. Just like the old Chinese saying: "A hundred types of flowers are blooming together.""

Many teachers commented on group dynamics in their assignments. They remarked that personalities, as well as academic skills, need to be considered in grouping.

"Every time I do the grouping, I pick out the group leaders first and ask them to recruit group members themselves. In this manner, the students in the same group usually have a solid friendship and group rapport. It's easy for them to communicate, and the learning environment is much more lively because of this."

––––––•––––––

"Generally, the groups form based on the students' learning performance and interest, as well as peer relationships (for instance, whether the students in the group can work together)."

Lessons from the West

Like their counterparts in China, the U.S. teachers used proximity control, and some mentioned it as a strategy to increase on-task behavior.

However, rather than discussing student movement, teachers were more likely to mention rearranging the classroom and reassigning seats. The difference in resource availability allowed these teachers to actually change the physical arrangement of their classrooms when student movement was warranted.

"I like working in groups. I very rarely work independently; it's always collaborative, so when I need smaller groups, the tables get separated. When I moved [into this classroom], I kind of shanghaied a couple extra tables because there weren't as many in here. [I did that] so there were different spaces we could move to [and be] comfortable."

U.S. teachers also used grouping to increase student engagement, and they again mentioned how resources and their classroom were modified to accommodate that movement.

"I use a lot of cooperative learning activities with high student engagement. There's less downtime and fewer behavior problems. I use a lot of Kagan's strategies. It's important to learn that you can depend on someone else to help you. This helps with discipline, too."

———◆———

"I think the most important thing is small-group instruction. I set up the classroom so the kids have a space to work. I also set up the class so the kids know where to get materials they need for learning. I want kids to be able to get what they need. Every person has a job so the classroom runs smoothly. I want them to be independent and functioning."

Some teachers noted the importance of allowing student input in the formation of groups. Though teachers in both countries tended to be teacher-directed in the control of their classrooms, use of small groups provided some student control and was evident in both countries.

"I have older kids, so some of [the lesson] will be guided instruction, and then there has to be a time when they can break off in groups and I have to use the classroom. The groups work well together. I have the groups at the beginning of the class tell me who they would like to work with and who they absolutely could not work with because—you don't know—yesterday's lover could be today's most hated person. So I . . . give them that autonomy to move in groups so they are in charge . . . after I've established some ground rules and after I'm pretty secure in sending them off with a task and they're going to do it."

Teachers in both countries used questioning to maintain students' attention, but the U.S. teachers offered more structured ways to ensure that they were monitoring quiet students.

"Then there's also the child that sits there quietly and is very good, but he doesn't have any identified special learning problems. He's working all night because he feels like he needs to, and he's really sleepy coming into class. I pay attention to those kids, too, because sometimes they need your attention a lot more than ones who are outwardly demanding it. I try to pay particular attention to very quiet kids who can get lost—so easily lost in all of this."

Practical Tips for Increasing Student Engagement

- Establish "bell work" that provides students with specific work to do as soon as they enter the classroom.
- Provide "anchor activities" that students can complete after they finish the regular assignment.
- Develop a plan for getting help so students will know what to do when they reach a learning roadblock.
- Use choral response techniques to increase student participation during whole-group instruction.

Lesson Tool: Kid Watch Cards

One way to make sure you're attending to all students in the classroom—and that no one can remain invisible—is to incorporate "kid watch cards" into your monitoring system. For a low-tech version, write a student's name on the bottom of each card. Arrange the cards on a clip board to create a flip chart (see Figure 5.1 for an example).

If technology is available, the format could be created in an Excel spreadsheet or something similar. Figure 5.2 provides an example of a form that could be used to monitor observations.

While monitoring the class, make individualized notes about students on their cards (be sure to date the entries). This information can be academic or social/emotional—whatever has captured your attention. These notes provide specific, personalized information that can be shared on report cards and in student conferences. When the cards are filled, replace them with new cards and maintain a file of all used cards. You will soon find that a pattern emerges. Some students' cards fill up quickly, whereas some remain quite empty. You can then adjust your focus to ensure students with blank cards are participating—by deliberate observation and strategically asking questions. Some students may be fine and are just

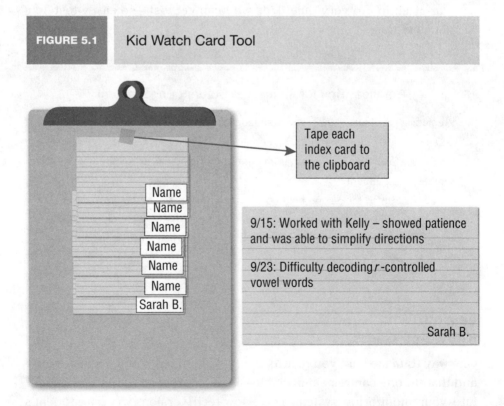

FIGURE 5.1 Kid Watch Card Tool

Tape each index card to the clipboard

Name
Name
Name
Name
Name
Name
Sarah B.

9/15: Worked with Kelly – showed patience and was able to simplify directions

9/23: Difficulty decoding *r*-controlled vowel words

Sarah B.

FIGURE 5.2	Monitoring Students Form

Student Name	Date	Observation	Date	Observation	Date

quiet by nature. However, some students may be struggling and are intentionally staying under the radar to avoid detection.

———————————— 教室聚光灯 ————————————

CLASSROOM SPOTLIGHT

The classrooms we visited in both China and the United States were marked by a climate of warmth and respect. Teachers demonstrated their caring for their students in a variety of ways, but a feeling of comfort and acceptance was immediately evident to us (relative strangers) as we entered the room for the first time.

In a Chinese middle school, students entered the auditorium (the only room with a projector, which the teacher needed for his lesson) and the teacher greeted his students warmly with a broad smile. It was clear that he was happy to be with his students, and the students smiled back. He listened to his students' questions and responded with respect and obvious caring. The students appeared comfortable experimenting with the materials provided as they explored the concept of lift in their physics class. Soft laughter was sometimes heard as the exploration and conversation between the teacher and class continued through the lesson. When the class was dismissed, they left with smiles and respectful bows as they departed the classroom.

In a U.S. class, 10 4th and 5th graders arrived and selected their own seats from among the three round tables in the classroom. The teacher began the class by asking if anyone had anything exciting to share. One student shared that he had learned that Adolf Hitler was suspected of living in South America where his own family had come from. Another shared that her grandmother had returned from a visit to Greece. A third student told the class that he was going to Hershey, Pennsylvania, on a family trip. Another student was going to Texas during the upcoming break. The teacher asked another student if there was good news about his family after a recent wildfire. The student explained that his cousin's neighbor had lost her home to the fire and there was a foot of ash covering everything. The teacher asked, "Has your cousin been evacuated? Is everyone safe?" The concern in her voice and face was evident, and the student assured her that the family was fine.

Lesson 3: Engage in Positive Discipline and Develop Respectful Relationships

To begin this lesson, we think it's fitting to relate the following quote:

> I have come to the frightening conclusion that I am the decisive element in the classroom. It's my personal approach that creates the climate. It's my daily mood that makes the weather.
>
> As a teacher, I possess a tremendous power to make a child's life miserable or joyous. I can be a tool of torture or an instrument of inspiration. I can humiliate or humor, hurt or heal. In all situations, it is my response that decides whether a crisis will be escalated or de-escalated, and a child humanized or dehumanized. (Ginott, 1972, p. 15)

Research studies have shown that effective teachers encounter fewer behavior disruptions than their less-effective colleagues. Figure 5.3

FIGURE 5.3	Intervals of Time between Incidents of Off-Task Behavior

	"Effective" Teacher *(top quartile)*	**"Less-Effective" Teacher** *(bottom quartile)*
Study 1	2 hours	12 minutes
Study 2	1 hour	20 minutes

summarizes the length of time between off-task behaviors as experienced by teachers in two studies (Stronge, Tucker, Ward, & Hindman, 2008; Stronge et al., 2011). Both studies showed that effective teachers spent much less time redirecting and correcting misbehavior among students. The award-winning teachers in our study had so few observable off-task behaviors that their classrooms provided further evidence that effective teachers spend less time on correcting behavior. We have already discussed the role that student engagement plays in reducing misbehavior. Beyond the "culture" of rules and procedures in classroom management, though, our teachers nurtured classroom climates that were safe, welcoming, and respectful. Proactive and positive discipline and positive student-teacher relationships were critical elements of such environments.

—————— 教师的想法 ——————

TEACHERS' THOUGHTS ON POSITIVE DISCIPLINE
AND RESPECTFUL RELATIONSHIPS

China / 中国

"For instance, I have been teaching for many years and have run into many challenging students. Some of them are not respectful and ignore you when you call them. They are very rebellious, but actually they are lonely and isolated."

"I do not directly criticize my students. If a student misbehaves, I smile at him and make eye contact to let him know that I know what's on his mind. If a student dozes off, I tell a joke to tease him (kindly). If students are whispering or talking to one another, I may call on them to answer questions. I usually do not criticize students in the classroom; instead, I give feedback on their behavior tactfully, so students can easily accept it, and we can address the problems after class privately."

———•———

"Having no behavioral problems in the classroom is impossible. When [students] are unable to focus on learning, there are two possible reasons: one is my teaching—they are getting tired of the way I present the material. In this type of situation, I make eye contact with them, and they will understand what I am trying to communicate."

United States / 美国

"I have empathy and understand what it's like to be that age. I'm very positive. Kids know I believe in them. Each day is a clean slate and we can start over."

———•———

"The praise aspect is important. One of the coolest things we do is a 'holla' [short for *holler*—shout-out]. When a kid gets a holla, I send an e-mail to the parents. I think it's really neat when a student or parent sends me a holla in return. I think that positive spirit is important. Being positive makes such a difference."

———•———

"They know I'm going to reward them for what they do well rather than be punitive, so they are not afraid to take a chance. That's my whole philosophy. Reward you for what you do well; it's all about positives. And then we'll build on those and then along the way maybe diminish the shortcomings."

Unfortunately, the modern interpretation of discipline usually means "punishment." However, the origin of the word has nothing to do with punishment. The word *discipline* comes from the Latin word *disciplina*, which means "teaching" and "learning." Therefore, in a strict sense, discipline is teaching—teaching right from wrong, about self-control, how to follow rules, and that other people have feelings and rights. Research has focused on the importance of proactive, preventative approaches to discipline, and education in the United States has recently been moving back to the original meaning of the word. An example of such research is Positive Behavior Interventions and Supports, which teaches students about expectations and the skills necessary to meet those expectations (Reinke, Herman, & Stormont, 2013). In addition, the use of punishment to change behavior is (finally) being called into question (Jones & Jones, 2012).

It seems as if our cadre of teachers knew intuitively what the research was showing. They didn't see student misbehavior as a personal affront; rather, they explored a variety of factors to try and determine why that behavior occurred, including looking at their own behavior and teaching. They believed that they had the power to change students' behaviors—not through punishment but by teaching, praising, and incrementally shaping new and more appropriate actions. Though there were subtle differences, much of what the teachers shared with us was consistent across cultures and will be shared in a joint lessons section.

Lessons from the East

The Chinese teachers explicitly discussed behavior in terms of morality (*dàodé* 道德). Moral behavior is a specific content that is taught, in addition to being embedded in other classes. One teacher commented, "We have an evaluation model to assess student learning and behavior. It is called '3 + X.' The 3 stands for moral behavior, learning, and physical fitness. The '+ X' means everything else."

A number of teachers considered it their responsibility to make sure students' behavior met the moral norms of the culture and to compensate for any perceived lack of parental support. They would make home visits and explain what parents needed to do for their children.

"The most challenging part of my job is dealing with the students who give me a headache and getting involvement from their parents. This aspect requires a lot of time and effort. Most of these kids are the only child in their family, and they are very selfish and stubborn, and sometimes they tell lies. It is very challenging to educate these kids, especially those who like to lie. Sometimes, it is difficult to communicate with certain children who have bad habits—probably due to their home environment. When you talk to them, you do not know if what they say is true or false. While interacting with these students, I need to lead them onto the right track step-by-step. This is difficult to do."

A second feature that was unique to teachers in China was the way they described how challenges were anticipated in their planning. They focused on instructional misconceptions and difficulties, as noted in the planning process described in Chapter 3. However, they did not directly discuss planning as a proactive way to avoid behavior issues.

Lessons from the West

Teachers in the United States did not explicitly connect behavior with morality. They also tended to be more accepting of diversity.

"I always try to find something important about my students, and I try to personalize them. I try to use their names. I try to pay attention to what they care about and make sure I say, 'Nice new piercing you got there' or 'Hey, you got some blue hair going on.' I think knowing your students and making sure that they know that you care about them goes a thousand percent to getting results from them."

In addition to understanding how the needs of their students affect behavior, teachers also tended to reframe parents' behavior. U.S. teachers don't have the same position of authority with parents as do teachers in China; therefore, they worked to be seen as equal partners rather than as an authority.

"Their parents love them and want them to succeed; they just don't know how. We have 19 new teachers on our staff this year, and I've heard so many times that 'Their parents just don't care.' And I say, 'Yes, they do.' 'But they didn't send them to school prepared.' I say, 'They don't have it at home.' They'll say, 'It's just a pencil.' 'I'll bet there are no pencils at their house. They probably packed up everything in a car last week and moved to that house. They left the pencils.' "

———————•———————

"One of the best places I go to interact with parents is yard sales. I like yard sales, but it makes me real to them, and it makes them real to me. When I go there, it puts me in a different place with parents, and we chat, and I always buy something. And then I believe they think I value them."

Joint Lessons Learned

Despite the lack of misbehavior observed during our visits, teachers in both countries acknowledged that challenging behaviors do exist. Runaways, conflict with parents, and classroom disruptions occur across cultures. These teachers, however, did not let misbehavior define their students or their relationship with their students. They maintained an overwhelming level of positive thinking and perseverance, and they demonstrated high levels of personal teaching efficacy. They believed that the combination of high-quality instruction, clear expectations and structure, and an atmosphere of respect and caring could chip away at the behaviors that prevent students from benefiting from the class. When asked what students at risk of failure need most, one Chinese teacher responded, "They need love most."

These teachers realized that even small gestures of caring can have a powerful influence on student success, especially when it is provided consistently over time.

"I had one student [who was disengaged and rebellious]. His entire family died in an accident, and only he survived. Since then, he lost his interest in learning and spent most of his time daydreaming during class. When I became the ban zhu ren of his class, I devoted a great deal of attention to him. I didn't take the straightforward way like talking with him face to face; rather, I sneaked to help him when he needed it. For instance, when winter came, I noticed that his clothes were too thin. I went out and bought him a coat and handed it to him without saying much. This touched him. We built a strong relationship since then. He started to think about the future, and he is a college student now." *(China)*

"Nowadays, some students are extremely disobedient. . . . In these situations, if you tell them, 'You are supposed to behave like this and this at home, and you are supposed to do this and this at school,' then they feel that your teaching intent is too obvious, and they won't listen. However, if you engage them in informal conversations, close the distance with them, and express your intention subtly, then they might accept you." *(China)*

"I'll take a behavior problem any day and they will be fine in my classroom, and they have been, so I've been able to prove that I can take any troublemaker and make him or her love school. It's my personal mind-set that I've been given a year with these kids, and it's my responsibility to make sure that they grow in that year—that they leave smarter and still excited about school." *(United States)*

Another element of creating the classroom climate these teachers used was praise and being positive. It permeated all of the interviews.

"I use praise [*biǎoyáng* 表扬] and positive feedback [*kěndìng* 肯定]. . . . I call the students who have strong logical thinking skills and are willing to take the learning to higher-level mathematicians. The students are really pleased with this title. Often, those who were called a mathematician tend to perform really well at the end of 9th grade, even though some of them might not have had a good start at the beginning of middle school." *(China)*

"If a student has a special interest or ability in another area, then we praise them and give them stars. . . . Previously, we only assessed student achievement. Although these at-risk students have academic achievement, it is not so high, and they have the opportunity to be praised in other ways." *(China)*

———————•———————

"My son used to accuse me of being pathologically cheerful. The poor kid was in my class, and he said, 'Gosh, do you ever cheer down, Mom?' That part has never changed. I'm just really positive and cheerful always." *(United States)*

———————•———————

"You need a positive attitude. The students are depending on you to learn. You set the tone. You need to leave your personal issues at the door and remember that the teacher is an important role model." *(United States)*

———————•———————

"I think that if we go to naming instead of shaming and blaming kids, right there we'll have an even stronger impact. [We need] to emphasize the importance of creating community ... and letting kids know. It's not just self-esteem like 'Oh, you're great, you're great, you're great,' but real self-esteem—where kids learn to evaluate and appreciate themselves for what their gifts are, for what their needs are." *(United States)*

Practical Tips for Using Praise

Researchers have recommended setting a standard of interacting with students at a ratio of four positive interactions to one negative interaction (Kalis, Vannest, & Parker, 2007). Here are some ways teachers can monitor this ratio:

- Keep a sticky note or index card on hand and record a tally of positives on one side and negatives on the other side.
- Ask a colleague to observe you and tally positives and negatives.
- Record your teaching so you can tally the interactions at a later time.
- Place a reminder in the classroom where you can see it frequently and think, "What is going well that I can praise?"

Slightly different from the positive approach, many of the teachers mentioned how they used humor and mutual respect to build relationships, engage and entertain students, and even diffuse potential conflicts.

"I always make the climate [of the classroom] more open, more pleasant. The students can play a joke on me. For example, my name is like the name of a vegetable, so I told the students they could call me a vegetable dish. In this way, I made the class happier." *(China)*

———•———

"Also, as a teacher, it is important to have a sense of humor. There was one time in the summer when one boy put his feet on the desk. You know, it was summer . . . and boys, their feet can be stinky. I approached the boy, patted his back, and said, 'Could you please not take your feet out of your shoes? They smell.' The student immediately put his feet down and laughed a little bit. The problem was humorously solved." *(China)*

———•———

"I make it fun. I laugh with them and sing with them and come up with silly dances for things that don't have silly dances with them." *(United States)*

———•———

"I respect my students as people and as individuals, and I value their choices and give them choices and say, 'We can do this and try that,' and really let them know that I'm trusting them with the information." *(United States)*

The relationship between teacher and students is key, and the teachers in our study nurtured the relationships needed to be effective. This brings us back to the beginning of this book.

"When I get someone new, the very first day I talk to that person and try to get to know a little about them and see where they fit in with the students. I start the relationship building from the very first day. The first day of school, I do not leave that period without knowing every student's name, so when they come in the next day I can call them by name. That's very critical to me." *(United States)*

—————•—————

"I can handle more conflicts, ask for help when I need it, and say *no* when I need to. I've developed an understanding of the culture and climate. I'm able to get these kids to produce despite the variety of their backgrounds. I can establish a positive relationship with the kids and help them feel comfortable in the class. They know that I'm on their side and I'm there to help." *(United States)*

—————•—————

"My students need to know a lot about me as a person to make [a positive relationship]. I shared my 3rd grade report card with them. Social studies was really hard for me, but I worked hard and went from a *D* to a *B*. I give my students the example that you have to give a lot to get a lot. If that's the only lesson some get, then I've made a difference." *(United States)*

Lesson Tool:
The 2 × 10 Strategy for Dealing with Difficult Students

Identify your most difficult student. This child is active, disruptive, and frustrating. Researcher Raymond Wlodkowski investigated a strategy called 2 × 10 and found it to be very successful with challenging behaviors (Wlodkowski, 1983). This strategy requires the teacher to focus on the most difficult student. For two minutes each day, 10 days in a row, the teacher has a personal conversation with the student about anything in which the student is interested (as long as the conversation is appropriate for school). Wlodkowski found an 85 percent improvement in that one student's behavior. What's more, the student will often become an ally for the teacher. In addition, he found that the behavior of all of the other students in that class improved. The student who receives the punitive consequences is often the student in most need of a positive connection with an adult authority figure. He or she needs that connection before being able to focus completely on academic content.

Summary

Jones (2009) posited that school leaders have begun to question the use of terms borrowed from industrial models. He suggested that schools abandon the term *classroom management* and replace it with *relationship building*. Teachers need to create a climate conducive to learning in the classroom. However, this is not a process to be managed, per se. The classroom is made up of a group of students who desire and deserve high-quality personal relationships with adults and peers. It is the quality of these relationships that drives their behavior and leads to learning. Figure 5.4 describes some differences when looking at the instructional climate as relationship building rather than as classroom management.

Jones could easily have been studying the teachers we visited when he created these identifiers for relationship building. The terminology mirrors the words our teachers used to describe their own practice. Classroom management and relationship building were not separate entities to these teachers; they were tightly interwoven in their practice. Teachers who build relationships with their students understand their students'

FIGURE 5.4	Classroom Management Versus Relationship Building	
	Classroom Management	**Relationship Building**
Classroom Rules	mandated	negotiated
Power	without question	with respect
Observation of Effectiveness	students are passive and quiet	students are actively engaged
Risk-Taking	discouraged	encouraged
Control Mechanism	negative feedback/ punishment	positive reinforcement
Primary Teacher Role	absolute attention	source of encouragement

Source: From *Strengthening Student Engagement* (p. 8), by R. D. Jones, 2009, International Center for Leadership in Education.

motivations and interest and build these understandings into their lessons, keeping students more engaged in their work and leaving less time to misbehave, which leads to greater achievement. Building a caring, respectful relationship full of trust allows students to feel comfortable taking risks and pushing beyond their comfort zones to achieve more than they might have thought possible. Teachers want to do their best to support their students, and students see their successes as a way to acknowledge and support their teachers. However, our teachers also demonstrated the management skills needed, not in the negative terms Figure 5.4 suggests as the traditional approach, but as the proactive skills of being prepared with organized resources. They had expectations and procedures that were clearly communicated to their students, and they had the experience to allow such skills to fade into the background so their instruction and learning could take center stage.

The spring rain moistens things silently.

This is a line from an ancient Chinese poem. The spring rain moistens things gently without making sound; similarly, teaching is a process that subtly influences students without leaving marks. This is certainly true when describing effective classroom management. It is interesting that both cultures have famous quotes related to teaching and highly related to classroom management that reference weather, seasons, and climate—perhaps reinforcing the appropriateness of using culture and climate as our framework.

6

Lessons Learned
第六章：借鉴经验

[Teaching is] like the spring rains, nourishing students bit by bit, and influencing them. Because spring rains moisten things silently, education should also be traceless, as stated by a famous educator. The less obvious the intentions of education, the more obvious the effects of education will be. —Chinese teacher

Teaching is like cooking. In a kitchen, you have an arsenal of tools and ingredients. Put together, they can create every dish imaginable. There are recipe books you can follow, and anyone can be a cook by following directions. But a chef understands the nuances and special character of each food and which tools and techniques will bring about the best flavors without consulting the cookbook. —U.S. teacher

We set out on a journey to uncover the beliefs and practices of great teachers in China and the United States. What began as a study focused solely on U.S. teachers evolved into this cross-cultural comparison. We had the great fortune to sit in some amazing teachers' classrooms and spend time talking with them about their work. In many cases, we ate meals with them, met others with whom they worked, and were welcomed by their students. In the United States, we visited teachers from the Pacific Northwest to the Southeast, from Pennsylvania to California and over to Illinois and parts in between. In China, we traveled from Yunnan Province to Shaanxi Province, from Beijing to Shanghai and down to Guangdong Province and parts in between. Throughout this extensive travel, we found what we set out to discover: lessons to be learned from these great teachers. We found lessons that cross the cultural divide and lessons that are germane to the cultural contexts in which the teachers were working. This final chapter provides a summary of those lessons, discusses some possible explanations for differences among teachers (based on their different educational and cultural contexts), and ends with illuminating metaphors created by teachers about teaching itself.

The Lessons

The most important lesson we learned is that great teaching is great teaching. It's as simple as that. In some of our observations, teams consisting of a Chinese and a U.S. researcher visited classrooms. In China, the Chinese researcher collected most of the observation data, since a language barrier prevented English-speaking scholars from knowing all that was said. Even so, the nonverbal cues evident in the classroom indicated a positive, productive, and respectful learning environment. In the United States, Chinese researchers had the same experience. Although one of the researchers may not have spoken the dominant language of a given classroom, the flow and interactions between teacher and student indicated something great was happening within those four walls. There are elements we observed in both China and the United States that are similar in personal characteristics, planning and assessment, instructional practice, and classroom management. We'd like to highlight a few of these similarities:

• **Personal Characteristics:** Teachers in both countries valued and worked to establish positive, productive relationships with their students.

• **Planning and Assessment:** Planning was viewed as a critical part of the teaching process, and assessment was included in that planning.

• **Instructional Practice:** Teachers used a variety of instructional activities at a range of cognitive levels.

• **Classroom Organization, Management, and Discipline:** The classrooms we visited were characterized by high levels of engagement with very little off-task behavior.

In short, these teachers could teach. With regard to "great teachers," it is often said that you'll know one when you see one. We saw 31 in two different countries. However, there were differences among the teachers, and some of those differences offer useful lessons and points of reflection for educators in each country. U.S. teachers can learn from how Chinese teachers think and engage in teaching and learning, and vice versa.

• **Personal Characteristics:** Teachers in China viewed teaching and learning as their personal responsibility to their children's families and to society as a whole. By contrast, teachers in the United States focused more on developing the individual potential of each child while having a strong impact on the overall educational system.

• **Planning and Assessment:** Collaborative planning was commonplace in China, and teachers engaged in peer observations. In the United States, planning typically took place in individual teachers' classrooms.

• **Instructional Practice:** Small-group work and individual teacher-student interactions were commonplace in the United States, whereas lectures and individual student work were more commonplace in China.

• **Classroom Organization, Management, and Discipline:** When dealing with behavioral concerns, U.S. teachers typically sought out reasons behind those behaviors, whereas Chinese teachers viewed appropriate behavior as a moral issue and focused on ensuring that students met cultural norms.

Figure 6.1 provides an overview of the similarities and differences between teachers in China and the United States. This figure and the previous descriptions serve to tell us "what is." What do effective teachers do in the United States and China? Beyond this, though, we were also interested in "why." Why were there differences in teaching beliefs and practices? Is it due to culture? Is it due to the structure of education? How might aspects of each affect what teachers do and how they think about teaching?

FIGURE 6.1 Similarities and Differences Between U.S. and Chinese Teachers

Aspect of Teaching and Learning	Lesson Similarities	Lesson Differences	
		China	United States
Personal Characteristics	• Positive relationships • A sense of purpose and responsibility • Sustained professional development • Self-reflection	• Familial relationships • Collective sense of responsibility to family and society • Collaboration and peer review as professional development	• Professional and community-based relationships • Focus on awareness of larger educational system • A variety of avenues for professional development
Planning and Assessment	• Planning based on curriculum and student learning needs • Focus on student assessment in planning process • Flexibility in carrying out lessons • Use of mental planning models	• Focus on anticipating student misconceptions in planning • Heavy reliance on textbook • Use of a uniform planning structure • Focus on collaborative planning	• Incorporation of assessment data directly into planning • Flexibility in use of text and supporting materials • Focus on individual planning
Instructional Practice	• Use of a wide variety of instructional strategies • High levels of engagement with the teacher as director of learning • High levels of flexibility and responsiveness • Differentiating learning • Stimulating learning environment	• High structure with extensive use of lecture • Intentional use of homework in teaching • Using tiered assignments for more advanced and struggling students	• More emphasis on small-group work and individual interaction with students • Student-centered focus of instruction • Use of varied grouping strategies to accommodate learners' needs
Classroom Organization, Management, and Discipline	• Effective use of available resources • High student engagement and on-task behavior • Positive discipline and respectful relationships	• Use of available resources and structure of classroom with high numbers of students • Focus on increasing student attention • Focus on behavior as morality and meeting cultural norms of society	• Use of classroom management in maximizing instructional time • Focus on rearranging the classroom to facilitate student movement • Focus on understanding source of behavior

The Cultural Context

In our study, we were interested in the similarities that would emerge across teachers in the two countries. However, we recognize that teaching and learning, as cultural actions, occur in specific cultural settings and evolve in ways that can reflect the underlying cultural values advocated and nurtured by the wider society (Leung, 1995; Li & Shimizu, 2009). Therefore, teachers' perceptions about the teaching process are influenced by general patterns in the culture in which they live and work. Hofstede's work on culture (see sidebar), including several ongoing studies of cultural similarities and differences, helps to illuminate the cultural dimensions and implications for teaching and learning. Figure 6.2 provides an overview of the six dimensions and how the United States and China rank according to those dimensions in the data from the Hofstede Center.

FIGURE 6.2	Cultural Values in the United States and China

Cultural Dimension	China	United States
Acceptance of Inequality Among People	*High Score* Accepting of inequality	*Low Score* Unaccepting of unequal treatment
Individualism Versus Collectivism	*Low Score* Highly collective culture	*High Score* Highly individualistic culture
Masculine Versus Feminine Orientation	*High Score* Highly masculine culture with a focus on success	*High Score* Highly masculine culture with a focus on success
Uncertainty Avoidance	*Low Score* Accepting of uncertainty	*Low Score* Accepting of uncertainty
Long-Term Orientation	*High Score* Focused on persistence and perseverance	*Low Score* Focused on short-term results

Measuring Culture

From the late 1960s into the 1970s, Geert Hofstede, a recognized Dutch researcher, conducted a large survey on national values among 117,000 IBM employees (from 55 countries) regarding people's behavior and how they collaborated. From the survey, four prominent factors emerged: power distance index (PDI), individualism index (IDV), masculinity index (MAS), and uncertainty avoidance index (UAI) (Hofstede, 1980). In 1991, a fifth factor or cultural dimension, long-term orientation (LTO), was added by subsequent researchers and based on data collected using a survey instrument developed with Chinese employees and managers. By 2010, the sample was expanded to 93 countries (Hofstede, Hofstede, & Minkov 2010). Figure 6.3 shows how the United States and China compare on the five cultural dimensions.

| FIGURE 6.3 | Hofstede's Cultural Dimensions |

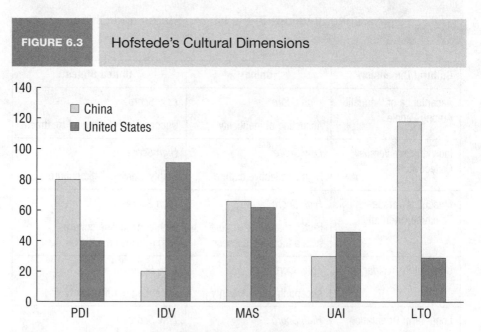

Source: Data from *Cultures and Organizations*, by G. H. Hofstede, G. J. Hofstede, and M. Minkov, 2010, New York: McGraw-Hill.

As is evident from Figure 6.3, general cultural patterns in the United States and China are similar on some of the dimensions and quite different on others. The United States and China are both characterized by a masculine culture—one that is success-driven and focused. In addition, ambiguity and uncertainty are accepted in both countries. In China, the superior-subordinate relationship is one that is accepted, whereas in the United States the role of superior-subordinate may be one of convenience or structure, but the two have different rights. Another striking difference between the two cultures is the Chinese focus on the collective versus a focus on the development of the individual in the United States. China is marked by perseverance and a future-oriented view of education, and the United States is focused on short-term outcomes. Much has been written about differences in student achievement, and much that has been said about those differences can be influenced by culture. In a research study that investigated the relationship between culture and student achievement, long-term orientation was found to be the most significant predictor of student achievement (Fang, Grant, Stronge, Xu, & Ward, 2013).

As an aside, we recognize that we seem to be making sweeping generalizations here about both countries. Schools influence—and are influenced—by what happens around them. Cultural norms based on long-established beliefs, values, expectations, and even hopes and desires blend to make teaching and learning what it is in any given setting with any given group of people. We would be naïve to suggest that one set of cultural norms is always superior to others or that a single set of cultural characteristics is best for students, but we can see the implications of culture on teaching and learning. At the very least, we understand that student success is directly influenced by the culture in which teachers and students live and breathe.

Cultural differences can be explanatory when viewing differences in beliefs and teaching practices. We found the following cultural aspects as major sources of differentiation between teachers in each country:

• **Philosophy of educational culture:** This philosophy is influenced by the focus on individualism in the United States and on collectivism in China. This could be seen in various schools' mission statements in each country. While visiting one school in rural China, we asked the school administrator about a sign on the wall. The sign was the mission of the school: "To serve the People." This focus on the capitalized *People* represents a focus on the collective. In schools in the United States, a typical mission statement may be to provide each and every student with the knowledge, skills, and values to be a lifelong learner, critical thinker, and contributing member of society. Such a mission statement is most often focused on developing the individual.

• **Views on the teacher-student relationship:** Teachers in China enjoy high social status, and students accept their teachers as their superiors. This is a reflection of the high value for power distance in Hofstede's cultural dimensions (see Figure 6.3). Teachers are held as moral role models. This is true in the Confucian tradition—the dominance of the teacher. In the United States, however, teachers do not enjoy an equivalent social status.

• **Cultural values:** In the Confucian tradition, filial piety (*xiào* 孝) is a philosophy in which respect for one's parents and ancestors is a virtue. Teachers transfer this filial piety to their classrooms. In the United States, teachers focus more on having respect for one another and on respecting diversity (see Figure 6.4).

The Educational Context

Structure drives behavior. A tenet of systems theory and systems thinking, this statement helps frame our discussion of the educational context within which these teachers work (Senge et al., 2012). Reflecting on our

FIGURE 6.4	Confucian Virtues Versus Western Characteristics

Confucian Learning Virtues	Western Learning Characteristics
• Sincerity • Diligence • Endurance of hardship • Perseverance • Concentration • Respect for teachers • Humility	• Individual thinking • Curiosity • Interest • Playfulness • Intrinsic enjoyment • Mastery

lessons learned with this in mind helps us understand how a system's structure affects teacher beliefs and practices.

- **Centralization of educational systems:** China's education system is highly centralized, from the curriculum to teacher training. When we visited Chinese classrooms, we were surprised by the commonality of phrases and ways that teachers described their beliefs and practices. A teacher in Yunnan Province, for example, described the three points of instructional planning in the same way as a teacher in Beijing described them. Two teachers, roughly 1,700 miles apart, used similar language to describe teaching and learning and engaged in similar practices. In addition, the use of national examinations makes the curriculum highly centralized and focused on that test. In the United States, historically, education has been decentralized, with educational systems as different as the 50 states. With recent education reform initiatives, such as No Child Left Behind and Race to the Top, there is more centralization in structures. However, we saw more differences among U.S. teachers—in terms of instructional activities used—than we observed among teachers in China.

- **Structural differences:** As mentioned in Chapter 2, Chinese classrooms are characterized by large numbers of students. Teachers teach more students but have fewer classes. In addition, they have more planning time than U.S. teachers do. The physical classroom is also a structure that drives behavior. In all classrooms we visited in China, the physical arrangement was the same—rows of desks tightly packed within a room. This was true of classrooms with 6-year-olds and classrooms with 14-year-olds. However, the number of students and the size of the available space made these arrangements necessary. Conversely, classroom structures in the United States were as varied as the number of teachers we observed. Some teachers had students arranged in a *U* shape, some had students sitting in small groups of four, and others moved students from the classroom carpet to individual desks. The number of students and the physical space influenced the differences we saw among teachers.

Final Lesson: Teaching Is . . .

Metaphors are powerful. They illuminate our beliefs and the connections we make between what we see and do and *how we think about* what we see and do. When we draw a metaphorical comparison, we are highlighting what we see as most important, and we are demonstrating how we make meaning of that concept. Thus, when we create a metaphor about teaching, we are showing something about how we think about teaching overall and what we find most important and salient about it.

Metaphorical thinking is culturally based. We develop metaphors based on how we live, where we live, our views of the world, and the natural environment that surrounds us (Li, 2010). Therefore, interpreting metaphors must occur through a cultural lens. Scholars have spoken of metaphors as a "way of talking about education in a language that brings with it a particular way of looking at the world (i.e., particular metaphors) and understanding what occurs" (Collins & Green, 1990, p. 71). There are many metaphors for teaching and education; such metaphors can be used for reflection, for changing practice, and for visualizing the teaching and learning process. Some common metaphors in the United States include the following:

- Teaching is coaching.
- Teaching is providing road maps.
- Teaching is growing flowers.
- Teaching is guiding.
- Teaching is conducting.

Indeed, metaphors have been used in teacher preparation to help preservice educators visualize the teaching and learning process and to uncover how veteran teachers think about daily practice in the classroom (Collins & Green, 1990; Wright, Sundburg, Yarbrough, Wilson, & Stallworth, 2003).

In China, metaphors are part of the culture and have been used to think about and uncover beliefs and assumptions about teaching and learning (Jin & Cortazzi, 2008). Some common metaphors in China include the following:

- Teaching is like a clear brook. (教学像一道清澈的小溪。)
- Classroom teaching is like an umbrella. (课堂教学就像一把雨伞。)
- Good teaching should look like a melodic symphony. (好的课堂教学就像一曲旋律优美的交响乐。)
- Teaching is cultivation. (教育就像是耕耘。)

Metaphors for teaching can explain the similarities and differences in how teachers visualize teaching and learning within and across cultures.

In our study, we asked teachers to create their own metaphors for teaching. Specifically, we provided these two prompts:

1. Create a metaphor that describes how you think about teaching.
2. How does this metaphor illuminate key aspects of your teaching?

The second question was very important. The responses to these questions uncovered some interesting findings regarding similarities and differences in how teachers think about teaching. Figure 6.5 provides a summary of the ways in which teachers thought about teaching.

FIGURE 6.5	Teacher Metaphors for Teaching

Teaching Is . . .	
U.S. Teachers	*Chinese Teachers*
a cycle and jazz song	a panda (*xióngmāo* 熊猫)
riding a roller coaster	jade without processing (*púyù* 璞玉)
a mother's heart	a relationship of love (*ài de guānxi* 爱的关系)
lighting a fire	playing an instrument (*tánzòu yùeqì* 弹奏乐器)
building a castle	watching flowers come into bloom (*kàn zhe huā kāi* 看着花开)
planning a party	a matchstick (*huǒchái* 火柴)
being a chef	a crutch (*guǎizhàng* 拐杖)
exploration	spring rains (*chūnyǔ* 春雨)
coaching	a bridge (*qiáo* 桥)
building a house	a wrangler (*mùmǎrén* 牧马人)
being a magician	performing a play (*biǎoyǎn huàjù* 表演话剧)
polishing diamonds in the rough	a song (*gēqǔ* 歌曲)
unlocking doors	planting a seed (*zhòng zhǒngzi* 种种子)
finding jewels in the rough	

Lessons from the East

"Teaching is like performing. You should know what your audience wants to know."

———•———

"Teaching is like raw jade without any processing, because the students have something that has not been developed or exposed."

———•———

"Teaching is like performing a play. For me, teaching itself is an art."

———•———

"Teaching is like growing a seed. You must have correct values like nutrition, a correct view of knowledge like sunshine, and correct methods like farmers' work."

———•———

"I think teaching is like a beautiful process of watching flowers come into bloom and listening to them bloom."

———•———

"Teaching is like a song. My students and I cooperate very well; we reach an integrated stage."

———•———

"I think teachers should be like spring rains, nourishing students bit by bit, and influencing them."

———•———

"I think teaching is like a crutch. It's like a guide for the students, but students should not keep using it all the time—otherwise it will break."

Lessons from the West

"Teaching is like coaching. It's really, really, really about the students, and coaches get that."

———•———

"Teaching is like a diamond in the rough—you know, something that you need to find and polish."

———•———

"Teaching is like cooking. In a kitchen, you have an arsenal of tools and ingredients. Put together, they can create everything imaginable. . . . But a chef understands the nuances and special character of each food and which tools and technique will bring about the best flavors without consulting the cookbook."

———•———

"Teaching is not standardization. . . . Teaching isn't teaching; teaching is facilitating."

———•———

"Teaching is like building a house. . . . Your need to take a look at what you have before you get there. You survey the land, you see where we're at, and then you have to bring in the materials and supplies that will make the house you want."

———•———

"I think of teaching as the lighting of a fire. It's striking passion in children. I think it's like riding a roller coaster. If you don't mind being on a roller coaster, it's the thrill of a lifetime."

Final Lesson Tool: Metaphor for Teaching

Develop your own metaphor for teaching. Ask yourself the same two questions we asked our teachers:

1. Create a metaphor that describes how you think about teaching.
2. How does this metaphor illuminate key aspects of your teaching?

By creating a metaphor for teaching, you uncover your own beliefs and how those beliefs influence your daily practice. After you've developed your metaphor, find a visual that depicts your metaphor. Then display that visual in your classroom or where you plan to remind yourself about your deepest beliefs about teaching. Two examples are below. One is from a Chinese teacher, and one is from a U.S. teacher.

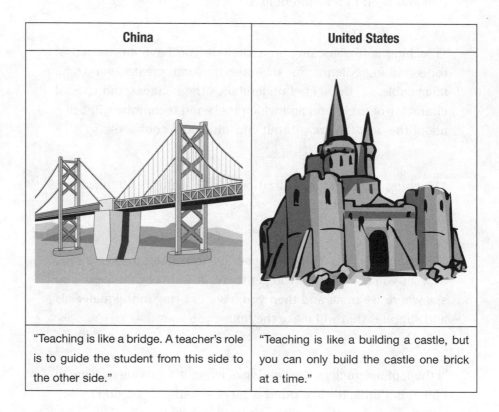

China	United States
"Teaching is like a bridge. A teacher's role is to guide the student from this side to the other side."	"Teaching is like a building a castle, but you can only build the castle one brick at a time."

Summary

Educational systems exist within cultures, yet it would be foolish of any one country to ignore promising practices from other places. With increased globalization, countries cannot ignore, or filter, the benchmarking of their students against students in other countries and other cultures. Although one could study the systems of education in both countries to explain differences in how students perform, at the center of the system is the truth that teachers matter. Internationally, this sentiment is echoed in the following quote: "The quality of an educational system cannot exceed the quality of its teachers" (Barber & Mourshed, 2007, p. 19). The lessons presented in this book allow for the sharing of ideas and best practices among the best that China and the United States have to offer.

References

引用

Alexander, R. (2002). *Dichotomous pedagogies and the promise of comparative research.* Paper presented at the Annual Conference of the American Educational Research Association, New Orleans, LA. (ERIC Document No. ED478168)

Allington, R. L., & Johnston, P. H. (2000). *What do we know about effective fourth-grade teachers and their classrooms?* Albany, NY: National Research Center on English Learning & Achievement, State University of New York.

An, S., Kulm, G., & Wu, Z. (2004). The pedagogical content knowledge of middle school mathematics teachers in China and the U.S. *Journal of Mathematics Teacher Education, 7,* 145–172.

Anderson, L., & Krathwohl, D. (2001). *Taxonomy of learning, teaching and assessing: A revision of Bloom's taxonomy of educational objectives.* New York: Longman.

Au, W. (2011). Teaching under the new Taylorism: High-stakes testing and the standardization of the 21st century curriculum. *Journal of Curriculum Studies, 43*(1), 25–45.

Bai, Y. (2000). Practices and characteristics of highly effective teachers. *Educational Research and Experiment, 4,* 31–37.

Baker, D. P., Goesling, B., & LeTendre, G. K. (2002). Socioeconomic status, school quality, and national economic development: A cross-national analysis of the "Heyneman-Loxley Effect" on mathematics and science achievement. *Comparative Education Review, 46*(3), 291–312.

Barber, M., & Mourshed, M. (2007). *How the world's best-performing school systems come out on top*. London: McKinsey. Available at http://www.mckinsey.com/ locations/ukireland/publications/pdf/Education_report.pdf

Berliner, D. C. (1986). In pursuit of the expert pedagogue. *Educational Researcher, 15*(7), 5–13.

Biggs, J. (1996). Western misperceptions of the Confucian-heritage learning culture. In D. A. Watkins & J. B. Biggs (Eds.), *The Chinese learner: Cultural, psychological, and contextual influences* (pp. 46–67). Hong Kong: Comparative Education Research Centre.

Blair, S. L., & Qian, Z. (1998). Family and Asian students' educational performance. *Journal of Family Issues, 19*(40), 65–72.

Bo, H. (2008). *A preliminary study on effective instruction of high school mathematics within the settings of implementing new curriculum*. Unpublished master's thesis, Shandong Normal University, Qingdao, Shandong, China.

Borko, H., & Livingston, C. (1989). Cognition and improvisation: Differences in mathematics instruction by expert and novice teachers. *American Educational Research Journal, 26*(4), 473–498.

Buttram, J. L., & Waters, J. T. (1997). Improving America's schools through standards-based education. *Bulletin, 81*(590), 1–5.

Cassady, J. C., Speirs Neumeister, K. L., Adams, C. M., Cross, T. L., Dixon, F. A., & Pierce, R. L. (2004). The differentiated classroom observation scale. *Roeper Review, 26*(3), 139–147.

Chan, C. K. K., & Rao, N. (2010). The paradoxes revisited: The Chinese learner in changing educational contexts. In C. K. K. Chan & N. Rao (Eds.), *Revisiting the Chinese learner: Changing contexts, changing education* (pp. 315–349). Hong Kong: Comparative Education Research Centre/Springer Academic Publishers.

Chen, C., & Stevenson, H. W. (1995). Motivation and mathematics achievement: A comparative study of Asian-American, Caucasian-American, and East Asian high school students. *Child Development, 66*, 1215–1234.

Cheng, V. M. Y. (2004). Progress from traditional to creativity education in Chinese societies. In S. Lau, A. H. H. Hui, & G. Y. C. Ng (Eds.). *Creativity: When east meets west* (pp. 137–168). River Edge, NJ: World Scientific.

Chudgar, A., & Luschei, T. F. (2009). National income, income inequality, and the importance of schools: A hierarchical cross-national comparison. *American Educational Research Journal, 46*(3), 626–658.

Coleman, L. J. (2006). A report card on the state of research on the talented and gifted. *Gifted Child Quarterly, 50*, 346–350.

Collins, E. C., & Green, J. L. (1990). Metaphors: The construction of perspective. *Theory into Practice, 29*(2), 71–77.

Conley, S., Muncy, D. E., & You, S. (2005). Standards-based evaluation and teacher career satisfaction: A structural equation modeling analysis. *Journal of Personnel Evaluation in Education, 18*, 39–65.

Cortazzi, M., & Jin, L. (1996). Cultures of learning: Language classrooms in China. In H. Coleman (Ed.), *Society and the language classroom* (pp. 169–206). Cambridge: Cambridge University Press.

Costa, A. L. (2001). Teacher behaviors that enable student thinking. In A. L. Costa (Ed.), *Developing minds: A resource book for teaching thinking* (3rd ed., pp. 359–369). Alexandria, VA: ASCD.

Crossley, M., & Waston, K. (2003). *Comparative and international research in education: Globalization, context, and difference.* New York: Routledge Falmer.

Cui, Y. (2001). Effective instruction: Concepts and strategies. *Platform of Teaching and Learning, 6,* 46–47.

Cui, Y., & Wang, S. (2005). Conceptualizing and constructing effective instruction. *Curriculum and Instruction in Elementary and Secondary Education, 182,* 5–7.

Danielson, C. (2007). *Enhancing professional practice: A framework for teaching* (2nd ed.). Alexandria, VA: ASCD.

Darling-Hammond, L. (2010). Teacher education and the American future. *Journal of Teacher Education, 61*(1–2), 35–47.

Deal, T. E., & Kennedy, A. A. (2000). *Corporate culture: The rites and rituals of corporate life.* New York: Perseus.

Dewey, J. (1916). *Democracy and education.* Boston: Macmillan.

Du, H. (2004). A discussion on effective teaching within the implementation of new curriculum. *Journal of Southwest University for Nationalities, 25*(7), 356–359.

Evertson, C. M., & Emmer, E. T. (2013). *Classroom management for elementary teachers* (9th ed.). Boston: Pearson.

Fan, L., & Gurcharn, K. (2000). The influence of textbooks on teaching strategies: An empirical study. *Mid-Western Educational Researcher, 13*(4), 2–9.

Fang, Y., & Gopinathan, S. (2009). Teachers and teaching in Eastern and Western schools: A critical review of cross-cultural comparative studies. In L. J. Saha & A. G. Dworkin (Eds.), *International handbook of research on teachers and teaching* (pp. 557–572). New York: Springer.

Fang, Y., Hooghart, A., Song, J., & Choi, J. (2003). *Roles in context—Examine staffrooms as sites for teacher learning in three cultures: China, Japan, and South Korea.* Paper presented at the Annual Meeting of the American Educational Research Association, Chicago.

Fang, Z., Grant, L. W., Stronge, J. H., Xu, X., & Ward, T. J. (2013). Investigating the relationship between culture and student achievement. *Educational Assessment, Evaluation, and Accountability, 25*(3), 159–178.

Feiman-Nemser, S. (2001). From preparation to practice: Designing a continuum to strengthen and sustain teaching. *Teacher College Record, 103*(6), 1013–1055.

Gardner, H. (1995). Cracking open the IQ box. In S. Fraser (Ed.), *The bell curve war: Race, intelligence, and the future of America* (pp. 23–35). New York: Basic Books.

Ginott, H. (1972). *Teacher and child: A book for parents and teachers.* New York: Macmillan.

Goor, M. B., Schwenn, J. O., & Goor, E. (1997). *Create more time to teach*. Longmont, CO: Sopris West.

Gronlund, N. E. (2006). *Assessment of student achievement* (8th ed.). Boston: Pearson.

Hamilton, L., & Stecher, B. (2004). Responding effectively to test-based accountability. *Phi Delta Kappan, 85*(8), 578–583.

Hattie, J. (2003). *Teachers make a difference: What is the research evidence?* Retrieved from http://www.educationalleaders.govt.nz/Pedagogy-and-assessment/Building-effective-learning-environments/Teachers-Make-a-Difference-What-is-the-Research-Evidence

Hau, K. T., & Salili, F. (1991). Structure and semantic differential placement of specific causes: Academic causal attributions by Chinese students in Hong Kong. *International Journal of Psychology, 26,* 175–193.

Haynie, G. (2006, April). *Effective biology teaching: A value-added instructional improvement analysis model*. Retrieved from http://www.wcpss.net/results/reports/2006/0528biology.pdf

Hiebert, J., Gallimore, R., Garnier, H., Givvin, K. B., Hollingsworth, H., Jacobs, et al. (2003). *Teaching mathematics in seven countries. Results from the TIMSS 1999 video study*. Washington, DC: National Center for Education Statistics.

Ho, I. R. (2001). Are Chinese teachers authoritarian? In D. A. Watkins & J. B. Biggs (Eds.), *Teaching the Chinese learner: Psychological and pedagogical perspectives* (pp. 99–114). Hong Kong: Comparative Education Research Centre.

Hofstede, G. H. (1980). *Culture's consequences, international differences in work-related values.* Beverly Hills, CA.: Sage.

Hofstede, G. H., Hofstede, G. J., & Minkov, M. (2010). *Cultures and organizations: Software of the mind: Intercultural cooperation and its importance for survival* (revised and expanded 3rd ed.). New York: McGraw-Hill.

Huang, R., & Leung, F. K. S. (2004). Cracking the paradox of the Chinese learners—Looking into the mathematics classrooms in Hong Kong and Shanghai. In L. Fan, N. Wong, J. Cai, and S. Li (Eds.), *How Chinese learn mathematics: Perspectives from insiders.* River Edge, NJ: World Scientific.

Hurd, J., & Lewis, C. (2011). *Lesson study step by step: How teacher learning communities improve instruction.* Portsmouth, NH: Heinemann.

Ingersoll, R. (2007). *A comparative study of teacher preparation and qualification in six nations.* Philadelphia: Consortium for Policy Research in Education.

Jin, L., & Cortazzi, M. (2008). Images of teachers, learning and questioning in Chinese cultures of learning. In E. Berendt (Ed.), *Metaphors for learning.* Philadelphia, PA: John Benjamins.

Johnson, S. M. (1990). *Teachers at work: Achieving success in our schools.* New York: Basic Books.

Jones, K. A., Jones, J. L., & Vermette, P. J. (2011). Six common lesson planning pitfalls: Recommendations for novice educators. *Education, 131*(4), 845–864.

Jones, R. D. (2009). *Strengthening student engagement.* Retrieved from http://www.leadered.com/pdf/strengthen%20student%20engagement%20white%20paper.pdf

Jones, V. F., & Jones, L. S. (2012). *Comprehensive classroom management: Creating communities of support and solving problems* (10th ed.). Boston: Allyn & Bacon.

Kalis, T. M., Vannest, K. J., & Parker, R. (2007). Praise counts: Using self-monitoring to increase effective teaching practices. *Preventing School Failure, 51,* 20–27.

Kauchak, D., & Eggen, P. (2013). *Introduction to teaching: Becoming a professional* (5th ed.). Boston: Pearson.

Kennedy, K., & Lee, J. (2008). *The changing role of schools in Asian societies: Schools for the knowledge society.* New York: Routledge.

Kennedy, M. M. (2010). Attribution error and the quest for teacher quality. *Educational Researcher, 39*(8), 591–598.

Klem, A. M., & Connell, J. P. (2004). Relationships matter: Linking teacher support to student engagement and achievement. *Journal of School Health, 74*(7), 262–273.

Laurier, W. (2011). *Madeline Hunter's lesson plan format.* Retrieved from http://iicti-part1-fall2011.wikispaces.com/file/view/madeline+hunter's+lesson+plan+format.pdf

Leung, F. K. S. (1995). The mathematics classroom in Beijing, Hong Kong and London. *Educational Studies in Mathematics, 29,* 297–325.

Lewis, C. (2002). *Lesson study: A handbook of teacher-led instructional change.* Philadelphia: Research for Better Schools.

Lewis, C., Perry, R., & Hurd, J. (2004). A deeper look at lesson study. *Educational Leadership, 61*(5), 18–23.

Li, J. (2003). U.S. and Chinese cultural beliefs about learning. *Journal of Educational Psychology, 95,* 258–267.

Li, X. (2010). Conceptual metaphor theory and teaching of English and Chinese idioms. *Journal of Language and Teaching and Research, 1*(3), 206–210.

Li, Y., & Shimizu, Y. (2009). Exemplary mathematics instruction and its development in selected education systems in East Asia. *International Journal on Mathematics Education, 41*(3), 257–262.

Liu, S. (2006). *School effectiveness research in China.* Unpublished dissertation, Louisiana State University, Baton Rouge.

Liu, S., & Meng, L. (2008). *Qualities of good Chinese teachers: Perspectives from teachers, students and parents.* 2008 National Evaluation Institute Conference on Assessment, Evaluation, & Professional Learning Communities, Wilmington, NC, October 8–11.

Liu, S., & Meng, L. (2009). Perceptions of teachers, students and parents of the characteristics of good teachers: A cross-cultural comparison of China and the United States. *Educational Assessment, Evaluation, and Accountability, 21,* 31–328.

Liu, S., & Teddlie, C. (2004). The ongoing development of teacher evaluation and curriculum reform in the People's Republic of China. *Journal of Personnel Evaluation in Education, 17*(3), 243–261.

Lookabill, K. C. (2008). *A descriptive study of the impact of the planning time on the utilization of the National Council of Teachers of Mathematics process standards within the Algebra 1 and applied mathematics subject fields.* Unpublished doctoral dissertation, Huntington, WV, Marshall University.

Lucas, R. M. (2005). *Teachers' perceptions on the efficacy of curriculum mapping as a tool for planning and curriculum alignment.* Unpublished doctoral dissertation, South Orange, NJ, Seton Hall University.

Mangin, M. M. (2005). Distributed leadership and the culture of schools: Teacher leaders' strategies for gaining access to classrooms. *Journal of School Leadership, 15,* 4.

Marton, F., Dall'Alba, G. D., & Kun, T. L. (1996). Memorizing and understanding the keys to the paradox? In D. A. Watkins & J. B. Biggs (Eds.), *The Chinese learner: Cultural, psychological, and contextual influences* (pp. 69–83). Hong Kong: Comparative Education Research Center.

McEwan, E. K. (2002). *10 traits of highly effective teachers: How to hire, coach, and mentor successful teachers.* Thousand Oaks, CA: Corwin.

Mendro, R. L., Jordan, H. R., Gomez, E., Anderson, M. C., & Bembry, K. L. (1998, April). *Longitudinal teacher effects on student achievement and their relation to school and project evaluation.* Paper presented at the 1998 Annual Meeting of the American Educational Research Association, San Diego, CA.

Milken Family Foundation. (n.d.). *Milken Educator Awards: Criteria for selection.* Available at http://www.milkeneducatorawards.org/about/criteria-for-selection

Ministry of Education of the People's Republic of China. (n.d.). *Ministry of Education's memorandum on selecting and recognizing recipients for 2009 National Teachers/ Educators Excellence Awards.* Available at http://www.moe.gov.cn/publicfiles/ business/htmlfiles/moe/s7000/201212/xxgk_145783.html

Misulis, K. (1997). Content analysis: A useful tool for instructional planning. *Contemporary Education, 69*(1), 45–47.

Muijs, D., & Reynolds, D. (2003). Student background and teacher effects on achievement and attainment in mathematics: A longitudinal study. *Educational Research and Evaluation, 9*(3), 289–314.

National Board on Educational Testing and Public Policy. (2003). *Perceived effects of state-mandated testing programs on teaching and learning: Finding from a national survey of teachers.* Boston: Author.

Nystrand, M., & Gamoran, A. (1991). Instructional discourse, student engagement, and literature achievement. *Research in the Teaching of English, 25,* 261–290.

OECD. (2010). *Lessons from PISA for the United States: Strong performers and successful reformers in education.* Paris: OECD Publishing.

OECD. (2013). PISA 2012 results in focus: What 15-year olds know and what they can do with what they know. Available at www.oecd.org/pisa/keyfindings/pisa-2012-results-overview.pdf

Paine, L. W. (1990). The teacher as virtuoso: A Chinese model for teaching. *Teachers College Record, 92*(1), 49–81.

Panasuk, R., Stone, W., & Todd, J. (2002). Lesson planning strategy for effective mathematics teaching. *Education, 22*(2), 714, 808–827.

Parke, C. S., Lane, S., & Stone, C. A. (2006). Impact of a state performance assessment program in reading and writing. *Educational Research and Evaluation, 12*(3), 239–269.

Pearson, L. C., & Moomaw, W. (2005). The relationship between teacher autonomy and stress, work satisfaction, empowerment, and professionalism. *Educational Research Quarterly, 29*(1), 37–53.

Piccolo, D. L., Harbaugh, A. P., Carter, T. A., Capraro, M. M., & Capraro, R. M. (2008). Quality of instruction: Examining discourse in middle school mathematics instruction. *Journal of Advanced Academics, 19,* 376–410.

Preus, B. (2007). Educational trends in China and the United States: Proverbial pendulum or potential for balance? *Phi Delta Kappan, 89*(2), 115–118.

Reinke, W. M., Herman, K. C., & Stormont, M. (2013). Classroom-level positive behavior supports in schools implementing SW-PBIS: Identifying areas for enhancement. *Journal of Positive Behavior Interventions, 15*(1), 39–50.

Reinsvold, L. A., & Cochran, K. F. (2012). Power dynamics and questioning in elementary science classrooms. *Journal of Science Teacher Education, 23,* 745–768.

Roorda, D. L., Koomen, H. M. Y., Spilt, J., & Oort, F. (2011). The influence of affective teacher-student relationships on students' engagement and achievement: A meta-analytic approach. *Review of Educational Research, 81*(4), 493–529.

Rosenthal, D., & Feldman, S. (1991). The influence of perceived family and personal factors on self-reported school performance of Chinese and Western high school students. *Journal of Research on Adolescence, 1,* 135–154.

Salili, F., & Hau, K. T. (1994). The effect of teachers' evaluative feedback on Chinese students' perception of ability: A cultural and situational analysis. *Educational Studies, 20*(2), 223–236.

Sargent, T. C. (2006). *Institutionalizing educational ideologies: Curriculum reform and the transformation of teaching practice in rural China.* Unpublished doctoral dissertation, Philadelphia, University of Pennsylvania.

Schwille, J., Dembele, M., & Schubert, J. (2007). *Global perspectives on teacher learning: Improving policy and practice.* Paris: United Nations Educational, Scientific and Cultural Organization.

Scott, T. M., Anderson, C. M., & Alter, P. (2011). *Classroom behavior using positive behavior supports.* Boston: Pearson.

Sedivy-Benton, A. L., & McGill, C. J. (2012). Significant factors for teachers' intent to stay or leave the profession: Teacher influence on school, perception of control, and perceived support. *National Teacher Education Journal, 5*(2), 99–114.

Senge, P., Cambron-McCabe, N., Lucas, T., Smith, B., Dutton, J., & Kleiner, A. (2012). *Schools that learn: A fifth discipline fieldbook for educators, parent, and everyone who cares about education.* New York: Crown Business.

Shi, J., & Zha, Z. (2000). Psychological research on the education of gifted and talented children in China. In K. A. Heller, F. J. Monks, R. J. Sternberg, & R. F. Subotnik (Eds.), *International handbook of giftedness and talent* (2nd ed., pp. 757–764). Oxford: Elsevier.

Shim, S. H. (2008). A philosophical investigation of the role of teachers: A synthesis of Plato, Confucius, Buber, and Freire. *Teaching and Teacher Education, 24,* 515–535.

Simon, H. A., & Chase, W. G. (1973). Skill in chess. *American Scientist, 61,* 394–403.

Soh, C. K. (1999). East-west difference in views on creativity: Is Howard Gardner Correct? Yes, and no. *Journal of Creative Behavior, 33*(2), 112–125.

Soter, A. O., Wilkinson, I. A., Murphy, P. K., Rudge, L., Reninger, K., & Edwards, M. (2008). What the discourse tells us: Talk and indicators of high-level comprehension. *International Journal of Educational Research, 47,* 372–391.

Stepanek, J., Appel, G., Leong, M., Mangan, M. T., & Mitchell, M. (2006). *Leading lesson study: A practical guide for teachers and facilitators.* Thousand Oaks, CA: Corwin.

Stevenson, H. W., Lee, S., & Stigler, J. W. (1986). Mathematics achievement of Chinese, Japanese, and American children. *Science, 231,* 693–699.

Stevenson, H. W., & Stigler, J. W. (1992). *The learning gap: Why our schools are failing and what we can learn from Japanese and Chinese education.* New York: Summit.

Stigler, J. W., & Hiebert, J. (1999). *The teaching gap: Best ideas from the world's teachers for improving education in the classroom.* New York: Free Press.

Stigler, J. W., Lee, S. Y., Lucker, G. W., & Stevenson, J. W. (1982). Curriculum and achievement in mathematics: A study of elementary school children in Japan, Taiwan, and United States. *Journal of Educational Psychology, 74,* 315–322.

Stigler, J., & Stevenson, H. W. (1991). How Asian teachers polish each other to perfection. *American Educator, 15*(1), 12–21, 43–47.

Stronge, J. H. (2007). *Qualities of effective teachers* (2nd ed.). Alexandria, VA: ASCD.

Stronge, J. H. (2010). *Evaluating what good teachers do: Eight research-based standards for assessing teacher excellence.* Larchmont, NY: Eye on Education.

Stronge, J. H. (2011). *Teacher effectiveness = Student achievement: What research says.* Larchmont, NY: Eye on Education.

Stronge, J. H., Tucker, P. D., Ward, T. J., & Hindman, J. L. (2008). What is the relationship between teacher quality and student achievement? An exploratory study. *Journal of Personnel Evaluation in Education, 20,* 165–184.

Stronge, J. H., Ward, T. J., & Grant, L. W. (2011). What makes good teachers good? A cross-case analysis of the connection between teacher effectiveness and student achievement. *Journal of Teacher Education, 62*(4), 339–355.

Sue, S., & Okazaki, S. (1990). Asian-American educational achievement: A phenomenon in search for an explanation. *American Psychologist, 45*(8), 913–920.

Sun, C. (2004). *A study on effective classroom teaching under the background of new curriculum.* Unpublished master's thesis, Shanghai Normal University, Shanghai, China.

Taylor, L. M. (2004). *The power of time and teamwork: The impact of instructional planning time and collaboration on the effectiveness of lesson planning by classroom teachers.* Unpublished doctoral dissertation, Cleveland, OH, Delta State University.

Tienken, C. H., Goldberg, S., & DiRocco, D. (2009, October). Questioning the questions. *Kappa Delta Pi Record,* 39–43.

Tomlinson, C. A. (1999). *The differentiated classroom: Responding to the needs of all learners.* Alexandria, VA: ASCD.

Tomlinson, C. A. (2001). *How to differentiate in mixed-ability classrooms* (2nd ed.). Alexandria, VA: ASCD.

Tomlinson, C. A., Brighton, C., Hertberg, H., Callahan, C. M., Moon, T. R., Brimijoin, K., et al. (2003). Differentiating instruction in response to student readiness, interest, and learning profile in academically diverse classrooms: A review of literature. *Journal for the Education of the Gifted, 27,* 119–145.

Tomlinson, C. A., & Imbeau, M. B. (2010). *Leading and managing a differentiated classroom.* Alexandria, VA: ASCD.

Tsui, A. B. M., & Wong, J. L. N. (2009). In search of a third space: Teacher development in Mainland China. In C. K. K. Chan & N. Rao (Eds.), *Revisiting the Chinese learner: Changing contexts, changing education* (pp. 281–311). Hong Kong: Comparative Education Research Centre/Springer Academic Publishers.

Tweed, R. G., & Lehman, D. R. (2002). Learning considered within a cultural context: Confucian and Socratic approaches. *American Psychologist, 57*(2), 89–99.

U.S. Department of Education. (2001). *No Child Left Behind Act of 2001.* Washington, DC: Author.

U.S. Department of Education. (2012, November 8). *Secretary Arne Duncan's remarks at the Microsoft Partners in Learning Global Forum.* Available at http://www.ed.gov/news/speeches/secretary-arne-duncans-remarks-microsoft-partners-learning-global-forum

U.S. Department of Labor, Bureau of Labor Statistics. (2010). *Occupational outlook handbook, 2010–11 edition.* Available at http://www.bls.gov/oco/oco2003.htm

Wagner, T. (2008). *The global achievement gap: Why even our best schools don't teach the new survival skills our children need.* New York: Basic Books.

Walberg, H. J. (1992). The knowledge base for educational productivity. *International Journal of Educational Reform, 1*(1), 5–15.

Walsh, J. A., & Sattes, B. D. (2005). *Quality questioning: Research-based practice to engage every learner.* Thousand Oaks, CA: Corwin.

Wang, X. (2006). *New curriculum's vision for the development of teacher's teaching capacity.* Unpublished doctoral dissertation, East China Normal University, Shanghai, China.

Watkins, D. A., & Biggs, J. B. (Eds.). (1996). *The Chinese learner: Cultural, psychological, and contextual influences.* Hong Kong: Comparative Education Research Center.

Watkins, D. A., & Biggs, J. B. (Eds.). (2001). *Teaching the Chinese learner: Psychological and pedagogical perspectives.* Hong Kong: Comparative Education Research Center.

Wayne, A. J., & Youngs, P. (2003). Teacher characteristics and student achievement gains: A review. *Review of Educational Research, 73*(1), 89–122.

Wiggins, G., & McTighe, J. (2005). *Understanding by design* (2nd ed.). Alexandria, VA: ASCD.

Wlodkowski, R. J. (1983). *Motivational opportunities for successful learners.* Phoenix, AZ: Universal Dimensions.

Wong, H. K., & Wong, R. T. (2009). *The first days of school: How to be an effective teacher* (4th ed.). Mountain View, CA: Harry K. Wong Publications.

Wormeli, R. (2006). *Fair isn't always equal: Assessing and grading in the differentiated classroom.* Portland, ME: Stenhouse.

Wragg, E. C., & Brown, G. (2001). *Questioning in the primary school* (rev. ed.). New York: Routledge.

Wright, V. H., Sundburg, C. W., Yarbrough, S., Wilson, E., & Stallworth, B. J. (2003). Construction of teaching metaphors through the use of technology. *Electronic Journal of Integration of Technology in Education, 2*(1), 1–22.

Zhang, F. (2008). *Effective instruction and new curriculum.* Unpublished master's thesis, Inner Mongolia Normal University, Hohhot, Inner Mongolia, China.

Index
引用

The letter *f* following a page number denotes a figure.

About the Authors

关于作者

Leslie Grant is Assistant Professor of Education at the College of William and Mary, and teaches in the educational policy, planning, and leadership area. Her research interests focus on cross-cultural comparisons of teaching, teacher effectiveness, and assessment literacy for classroom teachers and educational leaders. Leslie currently serves on the board of directors for the Consortium for Research on Educational Assessment and Teaching Effectiveness.

James Stronge is the Heritage Professor of Education, a distinguished professorship, in the Educational Policy, Planning, and Leadership Area at the College of William and Mary. James's research interests include policy and practice related to teacher quality and effectiveness, and teacher and administrator evaluation. He is a founding member of the board of directors for the Consortium for Research on Education Assessment and Teaching Effectiveness (CREATE). In 2011, James was honored with the Frank E. Flora Lamp of Knowledge Award, and was selected in 2012 to receive the Millman Award from CREATE.

Xianxuan Xu is currently a postdoctoral research associate at the College of William and Mary. Her research interests include teacher effectiveness, professional development, and teacher and principal evaluation. She also focuses on international comparative analyses of teacher qualities and student learning in the United States and China.

Patricia Popp is State Coordinator for Education of Homeless Children and Youth in Virginia and a Clinical Associate Professor in the Curriculum and Instruction Area at the College of William and Mary. Her research interests include children and youth experiencing homelessness and other forms of mobility, students with disabilities, and teacher quality. Pat is past president of the Virginia Council for Learning Disabilities and the National Association for the Education of Homeless Children and Youth (NAEHCY), and she currently serves on NAEHCY's committee for the LeTendre Education Fund.

Yaling Sun is Professor of Education and Director of the Curriculum and Instruction Department at Yunnan Normal University, in Yunnan Province, China. She is also a Counselor of Yunnan Provincial Government. Yaling's research interests cover areas of teacher education, schooling counseling, and curriculum and instruction. In 2007, she was awarded an Excellent Teacher of Ed.M., a national teacher education program by the National Committee for Ed.M. Education.

Catherine Little is Associate Professor of Educational Psychology at the University of Connecticut. In 2012, she was recognized as a University Teaching Fellow. Catherine's research interests include professional development, differentiation of curriculum and instruction, and classroom questioning practices. She also directs and conducts research related to UConn Mentor Connection, a program for academically talented adolescents. Currently Catherine serves on the board of directors for the National Association for Gifted Children.

Related ASCD Resources

At the time of publication, the following ASCD resources were available (ASCD stock numbers appear in parentheses). For up-to-date information about ASCD resources, go to www.ascd.org. You can search the complete archives of *Educational Leadership* at http://www.ascd.org/el.

ASCD Edge©

Exchange ideas and connect with other educators on the social networking site ASCD Edge at http://ascdedge.ascd.org/

Print Products

The Art and Science of Teaching: A Comprehensive Framework for Effective Instruction by Robert J. Marzano (#107001)

Assignments Matter: Making the Connections That Help Students Meet Standards by Eleanor Dougherty (#112048)

Breaking Free from Myths About Teaching and Learning: Innovation as an Engine for Student Success by Allison Zmuda (#109041)

Changing the Way You Teach: Improving the Way Students Learn by Giselle Martin-Kniep and Joanne Picone-Zocchia (#108001)

Classroom Instruction That Works: Research-Based Strategies for Increasing Student Achievement, 2nd Edition by Ceri B. Dean, Elizabeth Ross Hubbell, Howard Pitler, and Bj Stone (#111001)

Insights into Action: Successful School Leaders Share What Works by William Sterrett (#112009)

Simply Better: Doing What Matters Most to Change the Odds for Student Success by Bryan Goodwin (#111038)

Transforming Schools: Creating a Culture of Continuous Improvement by Allison Zmuda, Robert Kuklis, and Everett Kline (#103112)

The Twelve Touchstones of Good Teaching: A Checklist for Staying Focused Every Day by Bryan Goodwin and Elizabeth Ross Hubbell (#113009)

Where Great Teaching Begins: Planning for Student Thinking and Learning by Anne. R. Reeves (#111023)

THE WHOLE CHILD The Whole Child Initiative helps schools and communities create learning environments that allow students to be healthy, safe, engaged, supported, and challenged. To learn more about other books and resources that relate to the whole child, visit www.wholechildeducation.org.

For more information: send e-mail to member@ascd.org; call 1-800-933-2723 or 703-578-9600, press 2; send a fax to 703-575-5400; or write to Information Services, ASCD, 1703 N. Beauregard St., Alexandria, VA 22311-1714 USA.